ENDING THE BLAME CULTURE

ENDING THE BLAME CULTURE

❖

Michael Pearn, Chris Mulrooney
and Tim Payne

Gower

Published by
Gower Publishing Limited
Gower House
Croft Road
Aldershot
Hampshire GU11 3HR
England

Gower
Old Post Road
Brookfield
Vermont 05036
USA

British Library Cataloguing in Publication Data
Pearn, Michael
    Ending the blame culture
    1. Blame   2. Errors   3. Fallibility   4. Victims – Psychology
    5. Scapegoat – Psychological aspects
    I. Title II. Mulrooney, Chris III. Payne, Tim
    302.1'2
ISBN 0 566 07996 8

Library of Congress Cataloging-in-Publication Data
Pearn, Michael
    Ending the blame culture / Michael Pearn, Chris Mulrooney, and Tim Payne.
        p.   cm.
    Includes bibliographical references.
    ISBN 0–566–07996–8 (hardcover)
    1. Psychology, Industrial.   2. Errors.   3. Organizational behavior.   I. Mulronney, Chris.   II. Payne, Tim.   III. Title.
    HF5548.8.P37   1998
    158.7—DC21   97–45184
                                                                                        CIP

Typeset in Great Britain by Wearset, Boldon, Tyne and Wear and printed in Great Britain by Biddles Ltd, Guildford.

CONTENTS

❖

FIGURES

FIGURES

TABLES

PREFACE

❖

We all make mistakes and we all know how uncomfortable it is to get things wrong. It is embarrassing when others know of our mistakes and even worse when others punish us or try to make us feel bad about our mistakes. This is a deeply ingrained human experience that is common to us all. Yet it is surprising how rarely people speak freely about their mistakes. Maybe it is regarded as a mistake to speak openly about one's lapses, errors, omissions or commissions for fear of others taking advantage or seeking to disadvantage us where they have power over us.

Although mistake making is something generally to be avoided there is, at the same time, a recognition that sometimes mistakes can actually help us learn in a way that so-called sound advice or guiding principles or theory cannot. Clearly there are things that can be learned from experience, from trial and error, and from experimenting, that cannot easily, if at all, be learned any other way. Experience, just like experimenting, unavoidably involves making mistakes.

This book is about mistakes and what we can learn from them.

What do we know about making mistakes? What kinds of mistakes do people make? Where are they most liable to make them? What kinds of lessons do we learn from our mistakes? Are some kinds of mistakes more helpful to us than others? Can we learn to harness mistake making as a powerful source of learning? These are the questions we set out to answer in this book. The focus is primarily on individuals, though we also look at organizational mistakes and the implications for organizational culture.

The spur to this book was the opportunity to analyse a weekly series of 500-word articles that appeared in the *Independent on Sunday* newspaper over a five-year period. The articles were entitled 'My Biggest Mistake' and were written by eminent people, mostly from the world of business and commerce. The series was created and edited by Roger Trapp, to whom we are indebted for permission to analyse all the articles and to reproduce extracts in this book. We also gratefully acknowledge the permissions granted by the *Independent on Sunday*.

The great attraction of the series was that it presented real-life descriptions by people who had made real mistakes. This contrasted refreshingly with the usual servings of laboratory simulations where students (or rats) made mistakes under tightly controlled experimental conditions. Despite the limitations of the narrative accounts, it was an opportunity that was too good to miss. Roger Trapp previously published the first 100 articles with his own commentary.[1] By contrast, we subjected all 227 articles to systematic content analysis and used the findings as a springboard for this book. We hope they will provide both insight and understanding as well as practical tools and exercises to enhance the reader's capacity to learn from mistakes.

We also investigated the published research literature on mistake making both in individuals and in organizations. To our surprise there was very little formal research. The final pieces in the jigsaw came from our own research and developments in the field of organizational learning. Much of the practical material in this book is based on work we have done with our clients, and some of the examples we provide are drawn from the experience of organizations we have worked with.

Chapter 1 puts the case for the importance of mistakes as a source of learning and as an overview of the book. Most people feel and think about mistakes in a negative way. We illustrate this point with an analysis of the language used when describing mistakes. The negative associations discourage us from examining and learning from mistakes, both our own and those committed or perpetrated by others (note the language). We argue that a neutral non-threatening language is necessary if we are to optimize the benefits of learning from our mistakes. We describe the views of visionary leaders of organizations who recognize that making mistakes is not only desirable but essential for organizations to survive and thrive in the future. The chapter stresses the importance of learning from mistakes in the context of the recent emphasis, nationally and internationally, on lifelong learning and also the growing literature and thinking on the concept of learning organizations.

Chapter 2 examines in more depth the links between learning and making mistakes. We make a distinction between undesirable mistakes and intelligent mistakes, and develop the notion of mental models which are reinforced by successes but are only really challenged or changed in the face of undesired outcomes which are usually interpreted as mistakes. We briefly review the contribution of psychology to our understanding of the role played by mistakes in learning. The challenge for us as individuals and for organizations is to understand what lies behind our mistakes and to prevent their recurrence. The chapter contains two practical exercises to enable readers to achieve a better understanding of their mistakes.

Chapter 3 describes the detailed analysis of the 227 'My Biggest Mistake' articles. Having examined the strengths and limitations of the sample, we present a framework for recording the context in which the mistakes were made and the proportions falling into each category. This is followed by a practical exercise enabling the reader to assess the contexts in which they are most likely to make mistakes. The analysis moves on to the types of mistakes made by the authors of the articles. A framework for classifying the mistakes is presented, together with the proportions of the reported mistakes falling into each category. Illustrative examples and quotations from the original articles are used to give meaning to the classification framework. Finally, a practical exercise enables the reader to carry out a self-assessment.

Chapter 4 focuses on the lessons that the authors claimed they learned from their mistakes. We note the vividness and the strength of the language used. A classification framework is described, illustrated with examples from the articles.

Chapter 5 changes the focus from individual to organizational learning. We look at the concept of the learning organization and attempt to clarify the distinction between 'a' learning organization and 'the' learning organization. We describe how organizations can learn, and analyse the role that mistakes can play.

We analyse blame cultures and the pivotal role played by the attitude to mistakes which spirals downwards to fearful conformance and risk avoidance. By contrast, gain cultures, instead of fearing and suppressing mistakes, distinguish between different mistakes, discouraging some while tolerating or even encouraging others in the pursuit of innovation, change and improvement. Too great a fear, or a mismanagement of mistakes can lead to what has been called the three deadly Cs – conservatism, complacency and conceit – leading eventually to organizational stagnation.

The focus of Chapter 6 is on practical measures that organizations can adopt to enhance learning through better management of mistakes. One way is to audit the organization using the INVEST framework – **I**nspired learners (Are the employees motivated, willing and able to learn? Do they take calculated risks?); **N**urturing environment (Does it support and allow experiment and challenge?); **V**ision for the future (Is there one that people aspire to? Does the organization see itself as continuously learning in an unpredictable world?); **E**nhancement of learning (Does the organization systematically use techniques to enhance the learning potential and capabilities of everyone?); **S**upportive managers (Do they tolerate and learn from mistakes? Do they encourage challenge?); **T**ransforming structures

(Is cross-functional working encouraged? Do existing structures enable or even foster mistakes?). We also look in more detail at some of the techniques to enhance learning at the organizational level.

Chapter 7 is very practical with its main focus on individual learning and how to optimize the benefits of making mistakes. Ten techniques are described, many of them linked to practical exercises for the reader: (1) adopt a positive approach to making mistakes; (2) understand the difference between adaptive and creative (sometimes called generative) learning; (3) experiment as a powerful source of learning; (4) build your own conceptual models; (5) test your own assumptions and mindsets; (6) create support mechanisms for yourself; (7) question and challenge without antagonizing; (8) create personal learning contracts/plans/logs to manage your own self-development; (9) acquire a habit of active reflection, and (10) become a natural systems thinker.

Part of the positive management of mistakes entails seeking to break with convention within a framework which recognizes the possibility of getting things wrong as the calculated risk in seeking to do things better. Chapter 8 describes the learning spiral technique (introduced in Chapter 7) used in a group context. An example is presented in which a group of quality champions in a leading bank was given the freedom to shape its own development and learning needs over a twelve-month period. Among other things this entailed developing its own conceptual frameworks and models which it progressively improved and modified in the light of experience, rather than reacting to the models offered by the experts. Another example describes how a group of HGV drivers was given the opportunity to design and carry out a large attitude survey and consultation on its 400 peers in a sensitive and difficult environment. Neither management nor survey experts were involved. The result was a spectacular breakthrough in improved relations between the drivers and management.

A third example comes from a brewery where the workforce was encouraged to take personal responsibility for becoming active learners, one result of which was dissatisfaction among trainers and managers who preferred to tell and to control rather than react to energetically enquiring minds.

Involvement and trust are important issues if organizations are to harness the positive power of mistakes rather than succumb to the fear and punitiveness, the cynicism and passivity that hold sway when the experience of mistakes is entirely negative. Chapter 9 argues that consulting and co-creating are the essential ingredients of a gain culture. We attempt to summarize the book by itemizing thirty facts to remember (or at least know) about making mistakes. As a last flourish of potential usefulness we offer the reader a complete workshop design, 'Managing to Learn from

Mistakes'. It works well with groups but the individual reader can also benefit by flying solo through the exercises. It works even better if you can involve some friends or family.

FEEDBACK FOR THE AUTHORS

Writing this book was an adventure for us and many mistakes were made along the way. We may also have disappointed the reader by omission or commission.

To help us learn, and to rectify mistakes if we get a chance, tell us what you liked about the book and also what you did not like. There is a special form at the back of the book (p.207). We would be very pleased to hear from you.

Michael Pearn, Dublin
Chris Mulrooney, Oxford
Tim Payne, Oxford

July, 1997

REFERENCE

1 Trapp, R. (1993), *My Biggest Mistake*, Oxford: Butterworth–Heinemann.

CHRIS SWINSON'S BIGGEST MISTAKE

Chris Swinson is a national managing partner of BDO Binder Hamlyn. He read philosophy and economics at Oxford University before joining Price Waterhouse as an articled clerk in 1970. He left as an audit manager and in 1979 joined BDO Binder Hamlyn, initially as senior manager, technical services. He became national director of professional standards in 1988 and national managing partner the following year. He is chairman of the financial, reporting and auditing group of the Institute of Chartered Accountants. He has written five books.

My biggest mistake was turning up 24 hours early to temporarily replace a financial management team that hadn't yet been removed. In 1978 I was acting as an audit manager of a large company. Audit managers are the shock troops of a firm, ready to be sent at a moment's notice to the latest crisis or investigation.

Until then I had spent all my career in an accounting firm and my experience of practical management was insignificant. There were times when I longed for the responsibilities of a practical manager, rather than those of a professional adviser.

One Friday I received a request to go on the following Monday to a company I had not visited before. It was a small subsidiary of a large group. I was told that the group's management had decided to remove the subsidiary's financial management team. My job was to act as its chief accountant for two or three weeks until it was able to introduce a new team. My instructions were brief and limited, but my purpose seemed clear and I was looking forward to the experience. This seemed to me an exciting challenge, so it was with a sense of anticipation that I set out on the Monday morning.

On arriving at the company I announced myself boldly, but was a little disconcerted to find my visit was not expected. I found myself waiting in reception for rather a long time and conducting a deep investigation of the contents of a coffee machine. Eventually someone appeared to see me, and introduced himself as the subsidiary's chief accountant. After the initial, somewhat brief, preliminaries, he asked me exactly what I thought I was doing by turning up and announcing myself as the new chief accountant. Even though in those days I was green in judgement, I could tell that tact and diplomacy were now called for. As carefully as I could, I explained the instructions I had received and suggested that the best move might be for me to leave as soon as possible to sort out the problem. My suggestion was readily accepted. I returned to my office and during the afternoon the true story slowly became clear. I had arrived in the company's office a day early. The group's management had intended to announce the changes it had planned during that same Monday afternoon. No one at the subsidiary expected these changes to be made; my arrival was the first confirmation. Not surprisingly, the group's management was most annoyed that its carefully laid plans for announcing its decisions had been ruined by an inexperienced accountant who had received garbled instructions.

What did I learn from this? Firstly, I learned always to check my instructions, and often to double-check. I had not talked to the senior financial management team of the chief client group myself. Had I done this, it would have become clear to them that I had been told to arrive on the Monday. Since then I have never trusted relayed messages.

Secondly, I have learned to be more sensitive to the environment in which I find myself. The damage that was done by my abortive visit would have been mitigated if I had made sure of my ground before I went.

Finally, I have learned the importance of taking great care in dealing with a company's relationship with its people. My visit rendered the group management's objectives more difficult to achieve, and caused unnecessary distress to several people. I was not asked to return.

PART ONE

COMING TO TERMS WITH MISTAKES

❖

1

THE IMPORTANCE OF
LEARNING FROM MISTAKES

The greatest mistake you can make in life is to be constantly fearing you will make one.

Eldred Hubbard, *The Notebook* (1927)

There are two things that we can predict with 100 per cent accuracy about every person ever born. The first is that they will eventually die. The second is that during their life they will make mistakes.

Everyone makes mistakes. It does not matter how successful, clever, confident or knowledgeable you are. It does not matter whether you are a worldwide expert in your chosen field or a young child just beginning school. Making mistakes is an inevitable part of living. In fact life would be pretty boring if we never made them. Try to imagine how you would have to live your life if you were to avoid ever making a mistake. The words timid, cautious, insular, safe and boring come to mind. You would never be able to try new hobbies or sports, form friendships or loving relationships, go on holiday or take a new job, just in case it turned out to be a *mistake*. On the plus side, you may never need to experience that gut-wrenching feeling you get when you realize that 'something has gone wrong'. But on the other hand, you will never experience the satisfaction of things finally falling into place after a great deal of heartache; nor the feeling of discovering something quite exceptional by accident – as a result of a 'mistake'.

It is part of human nature to make mistakes. We are curious creatures who love to experiment, create and innovate; to take risks and push out the boundaries. By our nature, we will take several wrong turns to reach the right turn where we eventually achieve insight, invention and success.

Without these wrong turns life would be pretty dull. Nevertheless, mistakes have a bad name. We find it hard to talk about them. When we make one, we feel we have failed. To face up to mistakes and learn from them is extremely hard. Try Exercise 1.1, 'Thinking about mistakes' (p.17).

People on the whole are reluctant or unused to talking about their mistakes. During the course of our consultancy work with organizations we ask people to tell us about theirs, or to reveal them to their colleagues. Typical reactions are:

○   Do I really have to?
○   That's a bit embarrassing.
○   I'll have to think first.
○   No way!

We do not like facing up to mistakes because the experience is invariably unpleasant. We can feel embarrassed, ashamed, irritated, inconvenienced and threatened. If we make a mistake at home we may worry about how our friends and family will react. Will they laugh, make a joke, make fun of us, or get angry? If we make a mistake at work we may feel guilty for letting people down or for wasting time and money, and we may feel scared about what will happen if and when we are found out. This can cause us anxiety and can be career-limiting. Mistakes are bad enough when we are the only one who knows about them, but when they are made public we feel ten times worse, especially if we are then blamed, scolded or punished. On balance we prefer to keep our mistakes hidden. We are nervous of our own feelings and of the reactions of others.

But what is so wrong about hiding mistakes? Why should we drag them out, dust them off and submit them to detailed and painful scrutiny? What is the value of examining our mistakes? Consider the following situations:

○   The man who uses a washing machine for the first time, shrinks his partner's expensive new pullover and, rather than admit it, secretly buys a replacement.
○   The scientist who experiments by mixing two new chemicals, and creates a strange-smelling gas. Afraid of being reprimanded, she says nothing to her manager.
○   The military generals who planned the assault at the Somme in World War One. After the first attack, it was obvious to everyone that the strategy was suicidal. Afraid of losing face, the generals ordered their soldiers to continue.

In these three examples, the mistake-maker either hid the mistake or pretended it had not happened. Although they are different in the seriousness (or tragedy) of their outcome, these examples all illustrate the same point: if we do not examine our mistakes, we will not learn from them. In the first example, the man may have been embarrassed, or worried about his partner's reaction. He may have avoided an unpleasant scene, but he has not learned to use the washing machine. The second example could have more devastating consequences. When the scientist hides her mistake for whatever reason (fear, shame, ignorance), nothing can be learned. The gas released could be poisonous, or even very useful, but she will never know. The mistake may prove dangerous, but it will be too late to stop its consequences. It may well be repeated by someone else at a later date. The third example illustrates the price of not facing up to mistakes when in a position of power over the lives of others.

> The man who makes no mistakes does not usually make anything.
>
> William Connor Magee, 1868

These three examples emphasize that there is potentially great value in examining our mistakes and learning from them. The real value of mistakes is that we *can* learn from them. The problem is that we often do not. Indeed the lessons that we can learn from our mistakes may be very powerful; often they are lessons we could not learn any other way. The bottom line is that we *can* all learn from our mistakes – at home and at work. Consider the language used by people when they describe the lessons learned from their own mistakes (Box 1).

These quotes come from our analysis of the mistakes made and lessons learned by 227 well-known people. They were described in a series of articles in the *Independent on Sunday* in 'My Biggest Mistake'. We describe this research in more detail in Chapters 3 and 4.

OUR AGENDA

This book is about learning from mistakes; why it is important and how to do it. We may often fail to learn from our mistakes. See the downward spiral in Figure 1.1. Before we go any further, we would like to summarize our position:

O   Everyone makes mistakes.
O   Mistakes are usually seen as 'bad things', but in some circumstances they can be 'good things'.
O   The value in mistakes – the reason why they can be 'good things' – is that we can learn from them.
O   The lessons that can be learned from mistakes may be difficult to learn in any other way.

BOX 1   THE POWER OF LESSONS FROM MISTAKES

These quotes are from senior executives describing their own mistakes, highlighting the immense power of the lessons learned:

- It was a very hard, sobering lesson.
- We learnt the rough side of . . .
- It was extremely painful at the time.
- It started our belief that . . .
- It was a very good lesson in . . .
- It taught me a lot about . . .
- I learnt two lessons I will never forget . . .
- It taught me a hell of a lot of lessons.
- I should have done more . . .
- These days I . . .
- Next time round I made sure we didn't . . .
- Ever since, we have always insisted . . .
- I'm a jolly sight more careful now . . .
- The moral is . . .
- I was mortified, but I learned some important lessons . . .
- I learned always to . . .
- I now firmly believe . . .
- It taught me quite a lesson.
- I have never . . . since.
- I always begin by . . .
- You have got to . . .
- I was devastated. For the first time I realized . . .
- It sounded great in theory, but in practice . . .
- From now on we will stick firmly to . . .

- The way we feel, think and talk about mistakes is mostly 'negative'.
- This stops us examining and learning from our own mistakes, and also stops other people examining and learning from their own mistakes. It certainly stops us learning from each other's mistakes.

These points are important for everyone, in their personal and working life. Of course they have always been true, but we believe these ideas are especially relevant now because we live in an information society, where the ability to learn and to learn quickly is becoming increasingly important. Our own interests and professional activities are directed towards the world of work and organizations, so most of what we have to say applies

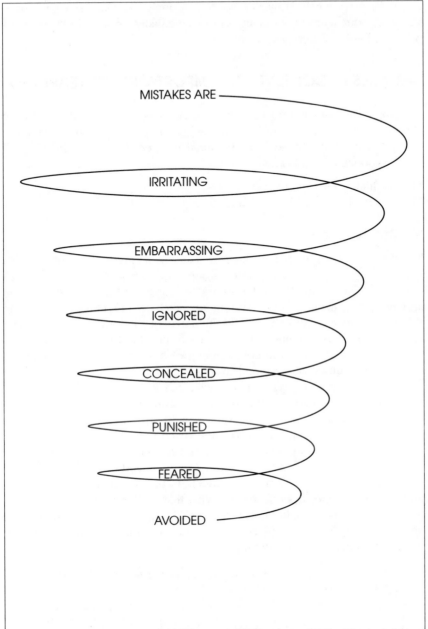

FIGURE 1.1   The downward spiral: why we fail to learn
             from mistakes

to the world of work. However, we feel strongly that the lessons we have learned about learning from mistakes are equally applicable to people's personal lives and personal development.

MISTAKES IN CONTEXT – THE IMPORTANCE OF LEARNING

Learning is fundamental to life; of this there is no doubt. In this book we will consider the importance of, and ways of learning from, mistakes in two particular life contexts: our personal life and our work life. We will now introduce two important topics:

○   lifelong learning
○   organizational learning and change.

LIFELONG LEARNING

The first global conference on lifelong learning was held in Rome in 1994, uniting people from fifty countries around the world. The year 1996 was designated 'European Year of Lifelong Learning' by the European Union and new organizations have sprung up, such as the European Lifelong Learning Initiative, and the World Initiative of Lifelong Learning. Some cities in Japan have identified themselves as 'cities of learning', and the G7 Nations have called for 'the development of human potential through the creation of a culture of life time learning'.

But what is lifelong learning, and what has it to do with mistakes? Lifelong learning is a vision for the future – a future where 'learning' does not stop when we leave school or college; a future where all citizens constantly strive to develop themselves and reach their full potential; a future where learning is fun, continuous and purposeful. It is an important vision, and is not just a 'nice to have'. With the speed of technological and social change ever accelerating, producing changes in the kind of work and leisure activities open to us, it is vital that we learn to learn, and continue to do so throughout our lifetime. Philosophers and poets have always known it; business leaders have recently understood it, and now even politicians have seen the light.

> The errors of young men are the ruin of business but the errors of aged men amount to this that more might have been done or sooner.
>
> Francis Bacon, 'Of Youth and Age', *Essays* (1625)

In this context, we need to grasp every opportunity and avenue of learning. We can read books, attend courses, use multimedia programs and 'surf the net'. But there is a more obvious source of learning which is available to all, every day throughout our lives. And it's free! This is the learning available from personal experience and mistakes, whether it be our own experience, or that of others. The need for lifelong learning only makes it more important that we learn to learn from *all* of our experiences. And that includes our mistakes.

ORGANIZATIONAL LEARNING

Until recently the organizations in which we work were fairly stable institutions. New ideas came and went, but mostly they carried on working in the same old way and they survived. Unfortunately this is no longer the case. Things are changing unbelievably fast. Organizations which invest in new products, production techniques or services find their competitors have copied and improved on them almost immediately. There is no longer any debate; to survive, organizations have to change, constantly and quickly. And in order to do this they have to maximize their capacity to learn (Box 2).

BOX 2   WHAT THE GURUS SAY

Two of the most enduring quotes from the management gurus illustrate the importance of organizational learning:

An organisation's rate of learning must be equal to or greater than the rate of change in its external environment. (Revans, 1982)[1]

The capacity of an organisation to learn may become the only sustainable source of competitive edge. (Stata, 1989)[2]

Much has been written about how organizations learn. Some people even talk about 'the learning organization' as if there were one and only one way to survive. However, most commentators emphasize the need for the people at the top of organizations to create an environment or 'culture' which rewards and encourages learning. They describe ways of helping people within organizations to share their learning, but they often fail to stress the positive power of mistakes. Mistakes have retained their bad name, even among learning organization theorists, until quite recently.

SUCCESS AS A POTENTIAL BARRIER TO LEARNING

Part of the reluctance to face up to mistakes is the preoccupation we have with success. There are dozens of studies and a massive array of books which attempt to capture the secrets of organizational success, either as a result of the philosophy and achievements of single individuals or of organizations. We can learn a lot from people and organizations that have experienced success over a long period of time.

Other books attempt to capture a formula for organizational success by examining a number of successful organizations. The aim is to extract the common factors contributing to their success. The most famous example of this approach in recent years is *In Search of Excellence* by Tom Peters and Robert Waterman.[3] The problem with this approach, however, is that many of the companies held up as examples of success eventually fail or hit hard times. Nonetheless there is an almost insatiable demand for books that offer the secrets of corporate (and personal) success.

Success is beguiling and attractive. In the short term it makes us more confident, motivated and satisfied. It empowers us to tackle problems with a renewed energy, and it *can* reward us personally and, in the short term, our businesses. However, there are dangers associated with success.

Organizations do not stay the same. To focus on past success and to rest on your laurels is to be complacent, to fail to learn; to die. As Richard Pascale put it: 'Whom the gods wish to punish, they first give 40 years of success'.[4] Planning a future based solely on what has worked in the past can be a dangerous course, as the case of IBM during the 1980s shows. It may ultimately be more profitable to focus on our mistakes than our successes. Only then can we be sure that we are learning, and moving forward.

THINKING ABOUT MISTAKES IS CHANGING

In many organizations, there is an almost morbid fear of making mistakes. As Patricia Sellers wrote in *Fortune Magazine*:[5]

> Most people view failure the way they do cancer – devastating, terminal, and too ugly to discuss.

Owning up to and talking about mistakes in the workplace is almost impossible. Conventional wisdom tells us that it is best avoided. In many companies, being associated with a mistake can result in others considering you to be incompetent, careless or a failure. The fact that you learned a valuable lesson from the experience is irrelevant. Rather than be asked to share your new-found wisdom with your colleagues, you are more likely to find your career severely limited.

On the whole organizations, like people in general, prefer success over failure. This fear of failure, however, can have some very negative effects. Think back to how a 'life without mistakes' would feel. Organizations that discourage mistake making can also be described as timid, cautious, insular, safe and boring. This can be a great problem for organizations operating in a world where competition can come from anywhere. The world is changing quickly and the only way for organizations to survive is to learn faster than their competitors, which is impossible without experimentation, creativity and innovation. But of course this inevitably leads to 'mistakes' being made, because when you try out something new it does not always work. Organizations that discourage mistake making become risk-averse. Punishing all mistakes also punishes and discourages creativity and experimentation. Employees are forced to cover up mistakes, so no one ever learns, and significant periods of time are spent 'reinventing the wheel'. The picture has been summarized by Mirvis and Berg:[6]

> In our culture failure is anathema. We rarely hear about it, we never dwell on it and most of us do our best never to admit it. Especially in organisations, failure is simply not tolerated and people avoid being associated with failure of any kind.

BLAME CULTURES

Many organizations around the world recognize what has become known as a 'blame culture'. Whenever a mistake is made at work, the immediate reaction is not 'How can we stop this happening again?' or 'Let's explore this problem so we can learn from it', but rather 'Who can we blame for this?'. We all have some tendency to blame what is outside our control when something goes badly: 'I would have run the marathon in four hours, but the wind was against me' (see Box 3). It is in our nature to be more comfortable if we can find something or someone else to blame for mistakes. Of course the end result of this is a climate of fear and secrecy, and a lack of innovation and experimentation. People play safe and try not to rock the boat. If anything goes wrong, they keep their mouths shut and cover up the mistake, or try to pin it on someone else. Organizations with a blame culture are unpleasant to work in and destined to underperform. However, thinking about the value of mistake making is beginning to change. Professor John Kotter from the Harvard Business School is famous for his work on organizational culture. He is quoted as saying:[7]

> I can imagine a group of executives 20 years ago discussing a candidate for a top job and saying: This guy had a big failure when he was 32. Everyone else would say, yep, yep, that's a bad sign. I can imagine that group considering a candidate today and saying, What worries me about this guy is that he has never failed.

Bill Gates, the founder of Microsoft, has said:

> I like to hire people who have made mistakes. It shows that they take

risks. The way that people deal with things that go wrong is an indicator of how they deal with change.

Bill Gates' argument is that people who have made mistakes in the past and (most importantly) learned from them make more successful leaders in times of rapid change. Put another way, do people who have not made mistakes make good managers and organizational leaders? Chris Argyris, another Harvard professor, goes further and argues that many chief executives get to the top of their organizations precisely because they *have not* made a big mistake. He believes that this can lead the business to underperform. Argyris says that such people focus the top team on safety, and avoiding mistakes, with the result that the organization stagnates.

BOX 3   THE FOUNDATIONS OF BLAME

An interesting study was carried out by two American researchers from Indiana University – Anne Sigismund Huff and Charles Schwenk[8] – who analysed speeches made by chief executives to financial analysts. They compared the speeches made in years when the organizations were doing well with those made in years when the organizations were doing badly. They found that the executives tended to *blame* poor organizational performance on factors outside of the organization, and outside of their control, for example the economic climate, trade legislation or competitor activity. However, when their organizations had done well, they took the credit themselves, and attributed the reasons for success to factors inside the organization and inside their control, for example good strategic decisions, good management or good people.

FROM BLAME TO GAIN

Writers on the subject have begun to distinguish between right and wrong types of mistakes. Managers at W.L. Gore, the manufacturers of Goretex fabric, make a distinction between 'above' and 'below' the line mistakes, taking an analogy of a ship (see Figure 1.2). If a hole is made above the water line of the ship, it is not a big problem, as long as you get it fixed before a storm comes. If you make a hole below the water line, the ship sinks. This is a very useful analogy, and makes an important point. We are not saying that all mistakes are good. We are not encouraging people to become careless or slapdash, safe in the knowledge that they will be able

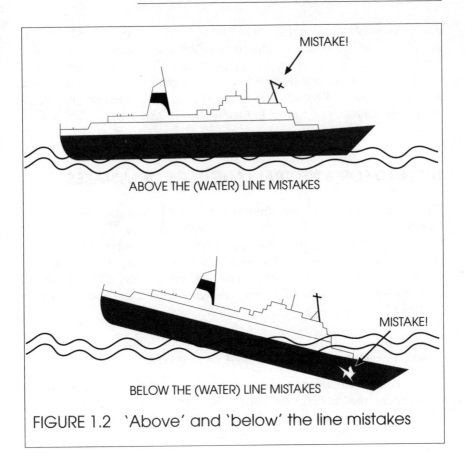

FIGURE 1.2 'Above' and 'below' the line mistakes

to learn from their mistakes later. Clearly there are some mistakes you do not want to happen ever. The examples of so-called 'rogue traders' illustrate the potential seriousness of big mistakes, or a series of uncorrected small mistakes. In some environments, for example those which are highly dangerous, highly regulated or highly sensitive, taking risks is not an option. In these cases, mistakes have to be made away from the workplace through simulations or 'games'.

It is clearly not a good idea for a bomb disposal unit to start experimenting with the way it defuses bombs. Picture the scene: 'I know cutting the red wire first always works, but let's check out what happens when we start with the blue wire.' This is definitely not an example of the right kind of mistake!

In most situations, however, 'intelligent' mistakes that stem from carefully thought out calculated risks can be most enlightening. To take advantage fully of the right kinds of mistakes, organizations need to move from a *blame* culture to a *gain* culture. By gain culture we mean one which is open and built on mutual trust and shared goals; one which encourages experimentation and respects the positive power of the 'right kind' of mistakes. (We explore the right kind of mistakes in Chapter 2 and discuss the gain culture further in Chapter 6.)

THE NEED FOR A NEUTRAL LANGUAGE OF MISTAKES

The language we use to talk about our mistakes is almost always negative (see Box 4). It is difficult to admit to and talk about our mistakes. This is because we feel threatened and upset by them. Using negative words makes us feel even more threatened. We need words which let us talk about our mistakes in a non-evaluative and neutral way. (This is exactly what we set out to achieve in our research on mistakes, and our results are described in Chapter 3.)

BOX 4   OUR CURRENT LANGUAGE OF MISTAKES

Our current language of mistakes is almost entirely negative. This heightens the anxiety and threat we feel when we think about mistakes, and makes it hard for us to talk openly about them. Here are some of the expressions we use when we are talking about mistakes:

O   mistake
O   failure
O   setback
O   negative outcome
O   blunder
O   disaster
O   slip
O   lapse
O   screw-up
O   blip
O   boob
O   error
O   cock-up
O   calamity

MISTAKES ARE VITAL FOR EFFECTIVE LEARNING

For people and for organizations mistakes are a vital part of learning from experience. Mistakes should be expected. In fact the absence of mistakes, or their disregard and denial, can seriously undermine effective learning for people in and outside of work, and for organizations as a whole. The absence of mistake making and the denial of learning which capitalizes on mistakes can ultimately stunt our personal development and threaten the survival of organizations. If we are to progress there must be experimentation and mistake making. This needs to be conscious, monitored, debated and, above all, talked about.

It is obvious that talking about and facing up to our own mistakes is not only uncomfortable but also dangerous. We tend to suppress open and honest discussion of our mistakes because we don't want to be labelled as a failure. But if we don't discuss them openly, we lose the power and the benefits of learning from mistakes.

WE NEED TO LEARN TO LEARN FROM MISTAKES

We need to learn how to face up to our mistakes. We need to see them positively and value the opportunity they present. In an era of lifelong learning we must grasp every learning opportunity that comes our way, and mistakes are among the most powerful. Of course this will require a change of attitude, both within ourselves and within organizations. We need to be able to talk about our mistakes without feeling embarrassed or that we have failed. We also need to be confident that others will support us in our endeavours.

Organizations must learn to capitalize on the lessons offered by making mistakes. In stable and predictable times there is less of a need to take risks, to experiment, or to break with tradition, all of which inevitably involve a higher number of mistakes. In times of rapid change, however, such as we have been experiencing in the last twenty years, experimenting, testing, and exploring new concepts and ideas are crucial to survival and continuing success. But how many organizations are well equipped to learn from mistakes? How many actually encourage testing and experimentation with new ideas? The answer to both these questions is 'very few', for two reasons. First, because the vast majority of people are not well equipped to face up to and learn from their mistakes. Second, most managers simply lack the skills to manage mistake making in a constructive way.

Mistakes are the natural result of experimentation. Their absence could mean that the organization and the people in it are not trying, or not trying hard enough, to find new ways to adapt and thrive in an ever-changing world. There is a risk that organizations, and the individuals that make them up, are playing safe and are doing today what they did yesterday, and will do tomorrow what they were doing today. When this approach lasts months, or even years, the organization is doomed to fail.

This chapter has examined the importance of learning from mistakes, both in helping us all individually to become lifelong learners, and in helping our organizations to cope with the rapidly changing world in which they operate. There are signs that thinking about mistakes is beginning to change, and we need to move from blaming ourselves or others to gaining from the positive power of mistakes. We need to learn how we can learn from our mistakes, and we argue that a neutral language of mistakes is essential if we are to move beyond blame and face up to our mistakes.

The next chapter examines in more depth the nature of the learning process and the critical role that mistakes can (and need to) play if individual and organizational learning is to be optimized.

REFERENCES

1 Revans, R. (1982), 'The enterprise as a learning system', in R. Revans (ed.) *The Origins and Growth of Action Learning*, Bromley: Chartwell and Bratt.
2 Stata, R. (1989), 'Organisational learning: the key to management innovation', *Sloan Management Review*, Spring.
3 Peters, T. and Waterman, R.H. (1982), *In Search of Excellence*, New York: Harper & Row.
4 Pascale, R.T. (1990), *Managing on the Edge*, London: Viking.
5 Sellers, P. (1995), *Fortune Magazine*, 6.
6 Mirvis, P.H. and Berg, D.N. (1977), 'Introduction: failures in organisation development and change', in P.H. Mirvis and D.N. Berg (eds) *Failure in Organisation Development and Change*, New York: Wiley, pp. 1–18.
7 Kotter, J.P. (1995), 'Leading change: why transformation efforts fail', *Harvard Business Review*, 73, 2, March–April.
8 Huff, A.S. and Schwenk, C. (1990), 'Bias and sense-making in good times and bad', in A.S. Huff (ed.) *Mapping Strategic Thought*, New York: Wiley.

EXERCISE 1.1   THINKING ABOUT MISTAKES

Think back over your life. Pick out one of the bigger mistakes that you have made, and think through the details. Write down a brief description of the mistake.

You may find these questions helpful:

> What happened?
> Where did it happen?
> When?
> What led to the mistake?
> Exactly what did you say or do that led to the mistake?
> How did you feel at the time?
> What, if anything, did you learn?
> What, if anything, have you done to prevent its recurrence?
> Have you made this kind of mistake since?
> Is there a pattern?

TONY FRAHER'S BIGGEST MISTAKE

Tony Fraher, 40, was born in Dublin. He trained as an accountant and joined the investment division of Bank of Ireland in 1971. In 1977 he joined Allied Irish Investment Bank as an investment manager, specializing in charity funds. He was made a board director and moved to London in 1983 to set up a UK investment division. In 1987 Morgan Grenfell asked him to set up its unit trust and retail division. He is a board director of Morgan Grenfell Asset Management and managing director of Morgan Grenfell Unit Trust Managers.

It's very important in business to research properly and do your homework. Yet you can be as prepared as you like and there's always going to be that one little item that you overlook – and it's rarely to do with business. This was the reason I made my biggest mistake.

It happened in 1980, when I was working as an investment manager with the Allied Irish Investment Bank in Dublin. I had developed a specialization in managing the investment of charitable funds. Before that the charities had their funds on deposit with the banks and I'd seen a market gap.

Most of the charities were religious and I found that I was acceptable to all denominations and charities both north and south of the border, partly because of my name. Gilbert Anthony Fraher is not an Irish name and while Gilbert Fraher is very much a non-Roman Catholic name, Tony was more acceptable to the Catholics. I never told anyone my religion.

In three years, from 1977 to 1980, I had cornered 83 per cent of the total market worth £300–400 million. Naturally our competitors were very keen to get in, but by 1980 I had most of the bishops, nuns, priests, Presbyterians, Christian Scientists – you name them.

But my moment of glory came with one bishop who I hadn't been able to move. For years I had researched and worked on him, and eventually he agreed to see me. A colleague and I were due to arrive one day at his home in the deep rural south of Ireland at 11.45.

Now I prided myself on the amount of homework and research I always did on every client, but I should have realized that the bishop was also doing his homework. He was used to talking to his local bank manager and here were these investment types coming down to see him. Not only that, but he was suspicious of my name and of my colleague who had a very Jewish name, although in fact he was a very devout Roman Catholic.

We arrived at 11.45 and were given a glass of sherry. We sat, going through the pleasantries before getting down to the serious stuff when, at noon, the angelus bell rang from the cathedral.

And something happened that had never happened before. For all my great preparation I had completely overlooked it. The bishop said, 'Let us pray'. He stood up, and in the shock so did I, knocking over the table, the sherry, my cigarette and the ashtray on his carpet. But he kept going.

My colleague was fine. He knew all the words and I mumbled my way through the first one. The angelus is the same prayer repeated three times, so by the second time I was getting the hang of it and could almost synchronize my words. But the bishop had spotted all of this, and when it came to the third one he threw me a complete wobbler. He changed to Gaelic and that totally destroyed me. I just looked at him, then I looked at my colleague and I thought, 'Oh dear'.

All of this took about three minutes and wiped out three years of research and work. The meeting endured for a further 10 frosty minutes whereupon we were informed that there was no interest in our services. Three days later we heard that our biggest competitor, who'd been looking for a toehold in the market, had been appointed investment manager to this bishop.

In Ireland Allied Irish Investment Bank still has a 63 per cent share of that market. But for the want of a Hail Mary I left a gap for a competitor.

2

FACING UP TO MISTAKES

This chapter considers the following issues:

○ Why put learning and mistakes together?
○ What do we know about how we learn?
○ What do we know about mistakes?

In Chapter 1 we argued that, as individuals, we need to learn and, in order to survive and thrive in the world today, we need to keep on learning. This is important not only for our employment chances, but also for our personal, intellectual and emotional development. When we stop learning we stagnate. We need to recognize that learning should not end when we leave school, college or university; neither should it be achieved solely through lessons, lectures, books or formal courses. Learning happens in everyday situations, even when we are not aware of it. Learning is a lifelong process which ends only when we die (see Box 1); until then, we are never too old to learn.

If this is true for individuals, then organizations must also learn continuously – organizations of all kinds: wealth-creating enterprises, public sector bodies and agencies, or less formal organizations such as communities and social groups. All must learn to do what they can already do, only more quickly and efficiently. They must also learn to do these things in new and innovative ways which satisfy all their stakeholders. Most importantly all organizations, indeed industries, must be able to learn to do new things otherwise complacency and conservatism set in, sometimes with disastrous consequences (see Box 2).

As the world changes more and more rapidly, and stakeholders

BOX 1   AN OLD DOG *CAN* LEARN NEW TRICKS

It is a myth that people can only learn when they are young. Evidence suggests that age does not decrease learning ability. Research in the UK by Professor Pat Rabbit shows that despite wide individual differences, many of us continue to learn effectively to a ripe old age (a key message is 'use it or lose it').

Some future-oriented organizations, such as B&Q, deliberately employ older workers as assistants in their DIY superstores. They find that these workers are more knowledgeable about their products, and deliver better customer service than younger people.

BOX 2   ONE OF THE WORLD'S COSTLIEST MISTAKES – THE CASE OF THE SWISS WATCH INDUSTRY[1]

In 1968, Switzerland had 65 per cent of world watch sales and 80 per cent of world profits. The watchmakers had been making watches for years and were clearly very successful at it. They had a clear understanding of what their customers wanted – a finely detailed, handcrafted mechanism, made of many cogs and other components: 'finely detailed works of art; elaborately and lovingly hand crafted'.

In 1967, a Swiss scientist had invented the quartz movement watch, which was many times more accurate than the mechanical variety. The Swiss watchmakers looked at it and, influenced by generation after generation of success as watchmakers, decided it would never catch on.

The Japanese and the Americans, however, were more open-minded, changed the way they made watches and adapted the new technology. At the time, they had virtually none of the world watch market. Ten years later they had almost 80 per cent, and the Swiss share had dropped to 10 per cent. The Japanese learned and adapted to new world conditions; the Swiss did not, with far-reaching consequences. However, the Swiss are now fighting back, once they realized that the watch was a fashion accessory rather than a piece of micro-engineering, but their world domination of the watch market is, by this time, a piece of history.

become more knowledgeable and more demanding, organizations must anticipate and adapt to the future. The only way to do this is to learn effectively.

None of these ideas is disputed, at least within the business schools and management consultancies. Whether they are really understood and truly believed by industrial leaders, policy makers, or by line managers is a different matter. Nevertheless our aim in this book is to describe how people in and outside of the workplace can learn more effectively – by harnessing the positive (as opposed to the negative) power of mistakes.

> Experience is the name we give to our mistakes.
>
> Oscar Wilde

WHY PUT LEARNING AND MISTAKES TOGETHER?

What have mistakes to do with effective learning? Surely mistakes are inherently 'bad' things, to be avoided wherever possible? How will making mistakes help me to learn better? First, by increasing the power of learning through mistakes and, secondly, by preventing avoidable mistakes.

OPTIMIZING LEARNING THROUGH MAKING MISTAKES

If you are asking these questions, you share an attitude which many people within the worlds of education, work and social policy also hold dear. Mistakes on their own are not inherently 'good'. They may add nothing to your understanding, skill or competence. They may even be detrimental; for example, in the way others perceive you (as 'clumsy', as 'a failure' or as 'lacking in judgement'). On the other hand, when the 'right' kind of mistake is treated in the appropriate way, some of the most powerful lessons that you can learn may emerge. This is the value of learning to learn from mistakes, and the principle holds true in many walks of life, from business to sport, relationships and the arts. But what are the 'right' kinds of mistakes? We will be looking at this more closely later in the chapter.

Another reason to put learning and mistakes together is *prevention*. We have mentioned the 'right' kinds of mistakes; there are also the 'wrong' kinds – the ones you don't want to happen, of which there are at least two kinds.

PREVENTING THE MISTAKES WE DEFINITELY DON'T WANT

The first kind of mistake we should avoid is a repeated mistake. By reflecting on and learning from our mistakes, we can prevent them from happening again. This is as true for individuals as it is for organizations. Individuals have habits, or 'normal ways of doing things', which we fall into and which lead us to make the same mistakes over and over again. The typist who always spells the same word incorrectly, and spends time correcting it with the spellchecker each time, provides a trivial example. Organizations often fail to learn, and so also repeat the same mistake time and time again. Consider the project team which goes over budget because it underestimated the time needed to negotiate. Unless the organization as a whole learns from this mistake, the next project team will have the same difficulty. Once may be unfortunate but twice, in the words of Oscar Wilde, is 'merely careless'.

The second kind of mistake that we don't want is the really huge one: the one that should not happen at all. The big mistakes that could change your personal life for the worse, bring down a company, or adversely affect the welfare of millions. By studying the mistakes of others in a systematic way, we can learn why and how such mistakes occur, and how to avoid them. The lessons provided by the derivatives trader Nick Leeson at Barings Bank were clear enough for other banks around the world to learn from, and so prevent similar occurrences. This has plainly not happened in all cases, as evidenced by the subsequent massive losses at the Daiwa Bank and Sumitoma Corporation.

In order to show exactly why mistakes are vital to learning, we will look at what has been learned over the years about the role of mistakes in learning. But first, we need to understand a little more about how we learn.

WHAT DO WE KNOW ABOUT HOW WE LEARN?

People have studied how we learn for many centuries. Greek and Chinese philosophers reflected on this issue; western philosophers, psychologists, educationalists and students of management have all devoted time and effort to understanding the process of learning.

Given all this, you might expect there to be a definitive 'answer' which describes accurately how people learn. Unfortunately this is not the case. There are many theories about how we learn, few of which can be considered 'wrong', and many of which are extremely useful in different situations. There is, however, no 'right answer' to the question.

We need to ask a different question: Which 'model' or 'theory' of learning is most helpful in a given situation or context? There follows a simple and practical description of how we learn. It brings together several traditional approaches, and indicates original references if you are keen to follow up the different sources.

THE STEPS OF LEARNING

BOX 3   LEARNING FROM A BASIC MISTAKE

A woman decides to leave her job as an engineer working with a large car manufacturer, helping to design motor vehicles. She sets up her own business as a freelance consultant, and soon she has several big clients. From her previous experience she understands that, when running a company, it is vital to look at the 'bottom line', that is, how much profit she will be making once she has paid all of her bills and other expenses. She has a picture in her head, a mindset or 'mental model', of how businesses work. She calculates that based on her fees and her expenses she will make a handsome profit, and will be able to take her partner on a long holiday to the Caribbean at the end of the year.

After three months her bank manager telephones unexpectedly. She is told that she has exceeded her overdraft limit by Ecu 10,000 and that the bank is taking control of her business. 'But how can this be?', she thinks. As far as she is concerned she is making a healthy profit. The bank manager explains that this is true on paper, but unfortunately none of her clients has yet paid her and so, in reality, she has no money. The manager goes on to explain that looking at the bottom line is very important, but that it is equally important to watch the cash-flow position of the business, that is, how much actual cash is coming in and going out. She had paid her bills, but had received no money.

The woman reflects on her mistake. She realizes that her initial understanding of the way small businesses work was incomplete. She needed to change her 'mental model' to include a consideration of cash flow. She realized that she had learned a valuable lesson from her mistake. Unfortunately, the majority of start-ups are not given a second chance to learn from this basic mistake.

The learning example in Box 3 is based on real-life experience. It illustrates the way mistakes can help us to review how we understand the world (our 'mental model'), and so change, refine and enrich our understanding: in short, to learn.

Researchers as far back as the 1930s have found that we all carry around in our heads many 'mental models' which describe how we understand particular aspects of the world. We may have a mental model of the perfect soccer team, the way a family should behave at meal times, or the way a manager ought to treat his or her staff. The important things about mental models are that:

○   we are often not aware of them (they are usually unconscious)
○   they influence the way we behave, even though we are not aware of them.

Studies in organizations have revealed that executives have 'mental models' of their company and the markets in which they operate.[2] Although they may not be aware of these models, nevertheless the models determine the decisions they make about the business. For example, a marketing director may decide to increase the advertising budget for a product with falling market share because he has a 'mental model' which says 'if you increase advertising, market share increases'. A different marketing director may have another mental model: 'Increasing the advertising budget will have little effect on market share if it falls as a result of the economy, as opposed to a new competitor entering the market.' The second mental model here is clearly more complex, and will be more useful in the long run. Great value has been found in helping managers understand their own mental models, which often reveal untested or inaccurate assumptions they were not aware of.

Figure 2.1 demonstrates the role of mental models in the learning process. On the basis of our everyday experiences, we form mental models of how the world works. These models help us to understand the world in which we live and to predict what will happen. Occasionally, however, we have a novel experience which does not fit our mental model, which could not be predicted. At this point we have two choices: to ignore the novel experience and pass if off as an exception, or to accommodate the new experience into our mental model, alter it and learn (see Box 4 for an example of this).

Mental models are extremely important to us all, as they guide our thinking and our actions. They are 'mental shortcuts', and they provide us with a way of handling all the information our brains have to cope with. As with any shortcut, they can be dangerous, especially if we are not aware of taking them. Mental models can lead to mistakes because they contain assumptions which may be true most of the time, but not always. This is why examining our mistakes for lessons and insights can be so profitable – the mistake helps to identify our assumptions. The Swiss watchmakers described in Box 2 clearly had a very strong 'mental model' of what a watch was, and what customers valued, and this prevented them from seeing the value of a different type of watch. The process of reflecting on the mistake enriches our understanding.

MISTAKES AND MENTAL MODELS – 'IF IT AIN'T BROKE, DON'T FIX IT'

Mistakes play a vital role in learning. When everything is going well, we feel no need to look for a new way to live or work. The old adage of 'If it ain't broke, don't fix it' seems to hold true (see Box 5). The value of mistakes is that they force us to re-evaluate our mental models of how the world works. The commodities trader who loses $1 billion will affect the prevailing mental model of financial control within the industry. The businesswoman who focuses on profit until she finds that cash flow has dried up will have learned a valuable lesson. Mistakes allow us to think more closely and more critically about how we understand our world. They also provide insights that could not be achieved if we were constantly succeeding. Indeed, the large Japanese manufacturers who first introduced kaizen and continuous improvement principles understood this well. Mistakes in these firms were not covered up, or punished, but were used as opportunities to improve the manufacturing process. Without mistakes it is diffi-

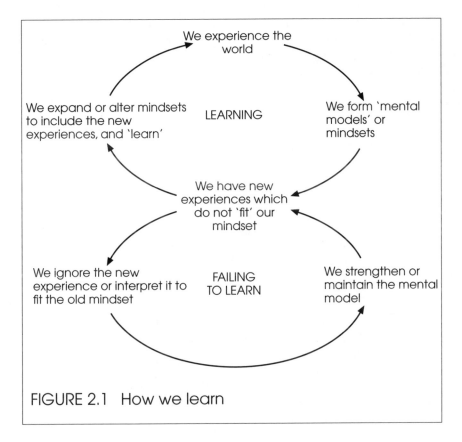

FIGURE 2.1   How we learn

BOX 4   MENTAL MODELS AND PREJUDICE

Prejudice is a good illustration of how mental models can guide our behaviour, even without us being aware of it. As we experience more and more people in the world, we find that some have various characteristics in common. It becomes convenient for us to think of these people as members of a group and we develop a mental model which describes them, albeit in a very general way.

Mental models of this type are often called stereotypes, and they can be reinforced by the way our media describe people. Examples of common stereotypes are:

- O   red-haired people have a strong temper
- O   Americans are loud
- O   English people are reserved.

These stereotypes can be positive or negative, although when we talk about prejudice we are usually referring to negative stereotypes. Someone who holds a strong stereotype of the kind 'the English are reserved', and then meets a wild and extrovert Englishman, may choose to reflect on the experience and learn (i.e. alter their stereotype). Alternatively, they may pass the man off as a rare exception, retain their stereotype, and not learn.

BOX 5   THE DANGERS OF SUCCESS

You might expect that years of succeeding would be a 'good thing'. Well, not necessarily. Harvard professor John Kotter studied a group of general managers, and their level of success. He writes:

> Because the [general managers] in this study were so successful, because they often had 20- or 30-year track records of win after win, many seemed to have developed an attitude of 'I can do anything' . . . when I asked hypothetical questions about the future, most answered in a way suggesting that they thought they could manage anything successfully . . .

Many people tend to remember the *positive* things that have happened, and take credit for them, whilst 'forgetting' the *negative* things. As Nick Leeson, the so-called 'rogue trader' who brought down Barings Bank, said: 'Some days I lost $25–30 million; some days I made $50 million. It adds to your belief that you can do it. It makes it easier to forget the debit and remember the credit.'

cult to evolve. Indeed, evolution *is* learning from mistakes. Mental models are thus at the heart of both learning and mistakes – they are the link between the two processes (see Figure 2.2).

MISTAKES ARE CRITICAL TO EFFECTIVE LEARNING

The case for mistakes seems clear. Learning is vital for personal and organizational development; mistakes are important because they help us

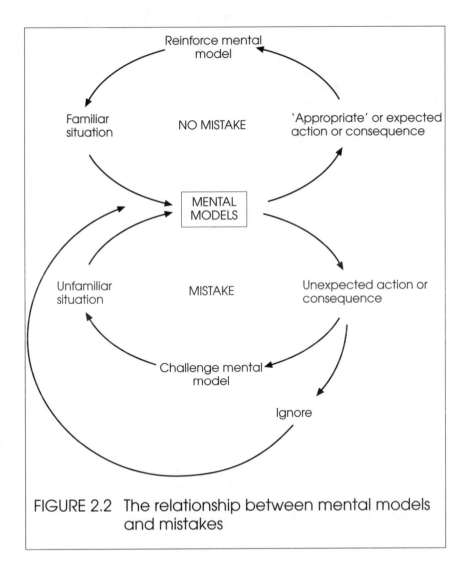

FIGURE 2.2   The relationship between mental models and mistakes

review the way we think about the world. Therefore, it is worth studying mistakes, to identify how best to make use of them.

WHAT DO WE KNOW ABOUT MISTAKES?

Many famous people have studied mistakes over the years, for example Sigmund Freud, Jean Piaget (see Box 6) and Hans Eysenck. We will begin, however, by trying to define what we mean by mistakes. A useful distinction, which provides our adopted definition of 'mistakes', is as follows:

○   *Mistakes* are planning failures. A person does something as they intended, without achieving what they wanted. For example, we might hit the wrong computer key because we incorrectly thought that it performed a particular function.

○   *Slips* occur when an action is performed which was not intended. For example, we might unintentionally hit the wrong computer key simply because it was next to the key we wanted to hit when we were distracted.

These ideas are very important. They make a clear distinction between 'planned' actions which later turn out to be mistakes, and mere slips which include accidents and lapses. In fact, slips are often associated with

---

BOX 6   THE CONTRIBUTION OF JEAN PIAGET[3]

The Swiss psychologist Jean Piaget began his working life studying children's IQ (intelligence) test performance. However, he soon became more interested in the mistakes they made when completing the IQ tests he gave them, than in their right answers. From his observations and studies over a long period of time, he developed a model of how children learn. He suggested that children learn through experimentation and play. By playing games such as knocking over a pile of building blocks, children began to learn about the world (for example, if you hit the building blocks, they fall over). Each new experience added a little to their knowledge of the world, and to keep their understanding of the world consistent with their new experiences, they adjusted their understanding. The idea of generating new experiences, experimenting and taking risks in order to challenge our existing notions, suggests an important role for mistakes to play in the learning process.

high levels of skill. When we can perform a set of tasks almost without thinking about it, for example driving a car, then we are moving into 'slip' territory. Slips are different from mistakes yet they still provide good opportunities for learning. Some of the mistakes reported in our research may be more accurately classified as slips. Nevertheless it is the 'planned' sort of mistakes with which we are most concerned in this book.

EVERYDAY ERRORS

The word 'error' has been used to mean all sorts of things. The *Penguin Pocket English Dictionary* defines error as: 'The state of being wrong'.

We can use 'error' as a catch-all term which includes our definition of mistakes and slips. Abigail Sellen has made a study of everyday errors through the examination of diaries kept by 75 undergraduate students.[4] She provides the following definitions:

O   mistake – an error due to an ill-formed intention
O   slip – an error in the execution of an intention
O   lapse – an error involving memory failures.

Sellen also describes various ways in which we can identify our own errors or mistakes, slips and lapses. We shall return to the subject of diagnosing our mistakes later in this book.

THE PROCESS OF MAKING MISTAKES

One person well known for studying mistakes is Dr James Reason, from Manchester University, UK. As he points out, it is a very human thing to make mistakes.[5] Many of the situations we face today at home and at work are extremely complex. We are constantly bombarded with information from TV, newspapers, radio, Internet, fax and telephone, and we only have so much space in our brain to deal with them all. Our brain has to simplify our tasks or objectives to make them more 'manageable'. When we do this we inevitably take 'mental shortcuts'. This process results in a number of common mistakes which in turn cause other, more familiar, mistakes. For example, Reason identified six of these 'mistakes which cause mistakes' (see Box 7).

They may not look, at first glance, like the mistakes most of us make. For example, what do they have to do with a mistake such as buying a used car which turns out to be a disaster; or with persuading your boss to try a new idea which doesn't work out? The answer is that these six mental shortcuts may be the reasons why we eventually make a mistake.

For example, imagine you are buying a used car. You fall instantly in love with the colour, the shape, the fact that it has a state-of-the-art

---

BOX 7   SIX MENTAL SHORTCUTS THAT CAUSE MISTAKES

James Reason has identified six underlying causes of mistakes:

1   A tendency to interpret information in terms of recent events, previous successes, and mindsets which have not been proven.
2   A selective examination of all the available information.
3   Inadequate time devoted to planning what should be done.
4   A low ability to assess statistical information which is linked to poor anticipation and prediction of future events.
5   A poor ability to work out the causal relationships between events.
6   Resistance to changing a course of action despite the availability of contradictory information.

---

radio/CD player, and the width of its tyres. You make up your mind there and then that 'I WANT THIS CAR.' More careful inspection reveals that the car is quite rusty, has been driven for over 200,000 km, and there is a dent in the bumper. 'TOO LATE – I HAVE DECIDED'. You buy the car. You have made a mistake. Why you have made a mistake is that you have resisted changing your chosen course of action (i.e. to buy the car), despite contradictory information (the rust, the mileage, the dent) – Reason's shortcut number 6.

Take the second example, that of persuading your boss to try a new idea and then finding out that it doesn't work. Imagine you have been planning to invest some of your company's money in a new business venture. When doing your research you remember that Jenny Holden, the 'star' of the company, recommended investing in an ostrich farm two months ago, and so far has gained a huge payback. You do some research and find three articles praising investment in ostrich farms. You also find two articles warning of the dangers, but you only 'skim' read these. You recommend to your boss that your company invests in ostrich farms. You have made a mistake. The reason this time is that first, you acted on the basis of what had been done before without critically examining this action. Even though Jenny Holden's investment appears to be doing well, it is still much too soon to tell. Second, you only examined a selection of the available evidence. You have three articles praising the investment, but two warning against it, yet you chose to concentrate on only the information which backs up your hunch, or mental model, that the investment will pay off.

TABLE 2.1   Process vs outcome mistakes

Process mistakes	Outcome mistakes
• Resistance to changing a course of action despite contradictory evidence.	• Purchasing a secondhand car that breaks down all the time. • A product that failed to gain market share.
• Interpreting information in terms of recent events and previous successes not proven. • A selective examination of all available evidence.	• A poor return on investment.

These examples illustrate the power of 'underlying' mistakes such as the six James Reason has identified. We have called them *'underlying' mistakes*, yet 'process' mistakes may be a more accurate term; they are the process which causes the outcome (investing badly, buying a poor secondhand car) that we call our mistake. Table 2.1 demonstrates the difference between process and outcome mistakes, with reference to the examples above.

Remember, it is the process mistakes which are more useful. It's useful for us to identify which of our mistakes are process mistakes. Try Exercise 2.1 (p.39) to help you do this.

Becoming aware of such mistakes has many advantages:

O   It lets us identify what caused our mistake in the first place.

O   It lets us identify something practical we can do to prevent the mistake, or a similar one, happening again.

O   It gives us a way of talking about the mistake which is less emotional – a 'neutral' language of mistakes.

This final point is very important because, as we have seen, emotion is one of the reasons why we tend not to discuss our mistakes and so not learn from them.

EMOTIONAL REACTIONS CAN LEAD TO A VICIOUS CIRCLE OF INCOMPETENCE

Chris Argyris, Harvard University, has been researching and writing about learning in organizations for many years. He observed groups of management consultants and other professions.[6] He found that the consultants often made mistakes. However, they not only failed to learn from them,

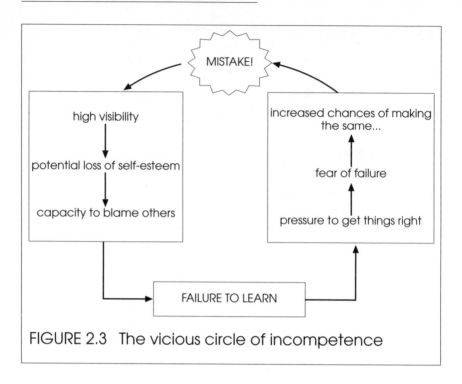

FIGURE 2.3 The vicious circle of incompetence

they did not even admit that the mistakes were theirs. Instead, they were keen to lay the blame at the door of others, i.e. their manager or their client.

Argyris found that they did not admit the mistakes, even to themselves, because of the anxiety and negative feeling created by such an admission. These people had high intellectual ability, were high achievers at work and had set themselves high standards. The idea of 'failing' was painful to them. Because they equated making mistakes with failing, they refused to entertain the idea that they might have made a mistake. This was the case even when senior managers provided a supportive environment in which to talk about what happened. If we do not reflect on our mistakes, we risk entering a 'vicious circle of incompetence' (see Figure 2.3), where we repeat mistakes again and again.

We are not so different from the high-flying management consultants. Since infancy we have learned to think of mistakes as failures, which results in a high level of anxiety whenever we wish to reflect on something we did. It can even be stressful to examine critically what we think we did well, let alone what we know we did badly. The result? We avoid thinking about our mistakes, and fail to reflect and learn from them. Similarly, we also tend not to analyse our successes in any depth, and so assume that what we did was the best we could have done.

The message is clear – to learn effectively from our mistakes we have to deal with the associated emotion. One barrier to this, as we noted earlier, is the language we often use to describe mistakes; a language which is invariably negative. Words such as 'accident, lapse, slip, boob, blunder and failure' are commonly used. The advantage of a set of 'underlying' or 'process' mistakes, which can be described in neutral, objective terms, is that it helps us to talk about our mistakes in a way which takes some of the emotion out of the situation. Try Exercise 2.2 (p.40).

WHAT ARE THE 'RIGHT' KINDS OF MISTAKES?

According to the research of Sim Sitkin, who is based in the Department of Management at the University of Texas, the right kinds of mistakes have six characteristics,[7] which are summarized in Table 2.2.

First, the actions which lead to them are *well planned*, which means that they can be repeated if successful, or varied systematically. Second, the *outcomes* of the actions are *uncertain*, so the right kind of mistake is like an experiment that turns up unexpected results. Third, there should be *neither too much, nor too little at stake*. No one would describe a well-planned experiment which sank the ship as the right kind of mistake! On the other hand, there has to be enough at stake for the outcome to matter. Fourth, there must be *rapid feedback* available – it is no good if you have to wait three years to find out whether or not you have made a mistake. Fifth, it must be possible to *adjust the actions quickly* on the basis of this feedback. So the right kind of mistake is not one that is unchangeable,

TABLE 2.2   Six characteristics of the right kind of mistake

1	Well planned action
2	Uncertain outcomes
3	Medium-sized risk
4	Rapid feedback
5	Actions can be adjusted
6	Relevant domain

like launching a nuclear missile for instance! Sixth, the action should be in a *relevant domain*. There is a limit to how far someone can go from their area of expertise for any error to be intelligent. For example, we would not be too hopeful that the right kind of mistake would result from a mathematics professor trying out a new kind of surgical technique!

Our view is that people, in all spheres of their lives, should be actively encouraged to make intelligent mistakes. We believe that the right kinds of mistake are among the most powerful learning opportunities available to us.

UNDERSTANDING PLANNING MISTAKES IN A COMPUTER-SIMULATED WORLD

Dietrich Dörner and Harald Schaub are two German psychologists who have conducted a long sequence of studies into the mistakes people make when planning and making decisions. Their studies use computer simulations of complex problems in which people have to take part. For example, in one simulation people had to govern a small computer-simulated town for ten years (not dissimilar to popular computer games such as SIM CITY), and the actions they took and mistakes they made were recorded and analysed. A second simulation involved business students managing the production, sales, investment and advertising strategy of a textile factory. In both of these simulations people were required to make decisions, the consequences of which they would have to deal with later on in the game.

Over several years, Dörner and Schaub have identified a set of 'underlying mistakes' that people make when playing their games (see Table 2.3).[8]

This set of 'underlying mistakes' helps us to examine and talk about our own everyday mistakes. Our research, which we will describe in Chapter 3, builds on this work. One of the reasons we continue to make mistakes is because we are unwilling to reflect on and evaluate 'how we have done' in the past. Our reluctance is because of the emotion associated with finding that we are not perfect after all, and might have made a mistake, which of course would not be good for our self-esteem. The main contribution of Dörner and Schaub, along with James Reason at Manchester University, is to help us understand that there are reasons for our mistakes other than our own stupidity. This makes it easier to discuss our mistakes and still leave our self-esteem intact.

We have highlighted the anxiety of talking about mistakes, and how this can prevent us learning from our individual mistakes. If it is this powerful for individuals, think for a moment how much more difficult it is to talk about mistakes when other people are involved. This is the challenge for organizations which want to learn from mistakes.

TABLE 2.3   Ten underlying mistakes

1	Not clearly defining your goals/objectives
2	Not managing to balance conflicting/contradictory goals
3	Being selective in the information you use
4	Entrenchment – getting bogged down in information
5	Oversimplifying the situation
6	Making predictions that ignore the complexity of a situation
7	Disregarding side-effects
8	Disregarding long-term effects
9	Not monitoring the effects of your actions
10	Not reflecting on your actions

In this chapter we have seen that there is much that is good about mistakes, providing we learn from them. There is of course a distinction between beneficial mistakes and those we don't ever want to happen, even once. We believe that making the right kind of mistake can be good for us, and not making 'intelligent mistakes' can be bad for us.

However, we tend to find mistakes difficult to talk about because we invariably link them with failure. We do not try to understand the reasons behind our mistakes and identify different types of underlying mistake. The research which we described goes some way towards helping us better understand our mistakes, and the important role they play in fostering learning.

The steps of learning show that mistakes can be seen as the unwanted side-effects of taking mental shortcuts. These mental shortcuts, most of the time, help us to deal with the complex world in which we live. So mistakes are not indicators of failure, but learning opportunities which can be capitalized on.

In our view, the challenge is to find a better understanding of what lies behind our mistakes and to learn to talk about mistakes in a neutral and non-threatening way. The bottom line is that we need to understand that the right kinds of mistakes are not failures. We set out to meet this challenge by researching the kinds of mistakes people make.

The next chapter describes our detailed analysis of the big mistakes described by 227 eminent people in the world of business and commerce. We present a way of classifying both the type of mistake and the context in a way that does not threaten the self-esteem of the individual.

REFERENCES

1 Barker, J.A. (1994), *The Business of Paradigms*, London: Harper Business Books.

2 Reger, R. (1990), 'Managerial thought structures and competitive positioning', in Anne Sigismund Huff (ed.) *Mapping Strategic Thought*, Chichester: John Wiley & Sons Ltd.

3 Piaget, J. (1951), *Play, Dreams and Imitation in Childhood*, London: Routledge.

4 Sellen, A.J. (1994), 'Detection of everyday errors', *International Review of Applied Psychology*, 43, 4, pp.475–498.

5 Reason, J.T. (1990), *Human Error*, New York: Cambridge University Press.

6 Argyris, C. (1990), *Overcoming Organisational Defences*, New York: Allyn and Bacon.

7 Sitkin, S.B. (1992), 'Learning through failure: the strategy of small losses', *Research in Organisational Behaviour*, 14, pp.231–266.

8 Dörner, D. and Schaub, H. (1994), 'Errors in planning and decision-making and the nature of human information-processing', *Applied Psychology: An International Review*, 43, 4.

EXERCISE 2.1 THINKING ABOUT DIFFERENT KINDS OF MISTAKES

Think of examples from your own experience. You may find it helpful to do this exercise in conjunction with a friend or close work colleague, taking it in turns to support each other's work. Try and think of at least three errors in each category.

Slips (an error in doing something that was correctly intended, e.g. dialling a telephone number)

```

```

Lapses (an error where your memory failed you, e.g. the name of someone known to you)

```

```

Process mistakes (where the plan or intention was wrong, e.g. reliable marketing data was ignored)

```

```

Outcome mistakes (where the intention was correct but the outcome was unacceptable or disappointing, e.g. a carefully chosen holiday was spoilt by exceptionally bad weather)

```

```

EXERCISE 2.2   UNDERSTANDING MY MISTAKES

STEP 1

When explaining why something you have done has gone wrong, what phrases do you typically use?

Do you use any of these?

It's always the same!
They never change!
They are all alike!
You can't trust anyone!

Write down the phrases you tend to use.

Now ask your close friends and colleagues. Write down the words they say you typically use.

STEP 2

Consider one or two of the more important (recent) mistakes that you have made. Now complete the following sections.

Mistake 1

What happened?

When and where did it happen?

What led to the mistake?

What exactly did you do (or say)?

Why, in your view, was it a mistake?

Mistake 2

What happened?

When and where did it happen?

What led to the mistake?

What exactly did you do (or say)?

Why, in your view, was it a mistake?

STEP 3

Now look at the phrases you use (or your friends say you use!), and also the reasons you give for the mistakes you described in step 2.

Is there a pattern? If in doubt, ask your friends and colleagues.

Q1   Are you interpreting events based on unproven views?

Q2   Are you selective (not attending to all the available information)?

Q3   Do you rush into things without careful (or sufficient) planning?

Q4   Do you tend to ignore quantified or numerical information when thinking ahead?

Q5   Do you fail to link things together, where one thing reflects another in a chain?

Q6   Are you reluctant to change your mind or your intended course of action even in the face of conflicting information?

If in doubt, or to test your own views, ask for your friends' or work colleagues' opinions.

EDWARD SIMONS'S BIGGEST MISTAKE

The developer of the Chelsea Farmers' Market shopping village, Edward Simons joined Harvey Goldsmith in 1983 to form Allied Entertainment. After winning two US video awards for *The Lawnmower Man*, he became involved in a $15m production of Nostradamus.

My biggest mistake was investing in a foreign business that I knew nothing about.

I was approached by an old friend last year with the idea of acquiring a minority interest in a Norwegian TV station. At the time Norway had four commercial stations, which, for a population of four million, was ridiculous. That, in fact, should have been a warning sign.

In April we put in $150,000 to acquire 26 per cent, which is far too cheap for a television station, but again, I didn't see that. Inevitably, about four weeks later, I had a call from the chairman in Norway, saying the company needed more money.

For a third time I should have realized all was not well, but although I was a little concerned, we were dealing with a very reputable firm of accountants and the figures looked very plausible. We had an option to acquire another 74 per cent, so the chairman came over with some advisers and we studied the balance sheets together.

By taking 100 per cent control, Allied could get an even better deal. That, of course, was the fourth mistake, because then we were completely sucked in. At that stage I committed a further $400,000. I went to Norway to have a really good look at the business, and at 7pm, when we were supposed to go on air, the screen went blank. They hadn't even put the tapes in. But on 1 August we took control and managed to turn it into a very professional operation. It would have been enjoyable if I'd had nothing else to do but be in Norway running a television station.

As it was, trying to run a business from more than 1,000 miles away was a nightmare that went from bad to worse. I was under constant pressure, receiving telephone calls from Norway in the middle of the night saying that they had run out of programmes to broadcast.

I never realized before what an enormous appetite a television station has. If you don't have programmes, you don't go on air, and if you don't go on air you don't have any income from advertising.

The final mistake was that we continued to drip-feed the station for a period of three months, at the end of which we had spent a total of more than $1 million.

By November we realized there was no hope of turning it into a profitable company and the only solution was to put it into liquidation.

The moment we took that decision it was like an enormous weight had been lifted off my shoulders. The whole experience was an unmitigated disaster. Looking back, it was a complete aberration on my part. I'm a reasonably good businessman – and a chartered accountant – but despite all the warning signs that were there, I was too caught up in the romantic idea of owning a television station to see them.

You should never invest in a business you know nothing about, nor should you attempt to run a company outside your own territory without installing first-class management locally.

We weren't even in the television business, yet there we were jumping with both feet into a foreign country.

If we were conservative before, we are much more cautious now – so cautious that Harvey (the late Harvey [Goldsmith]) says he's never going to let me out to lunch on my own again.

3

MISTAKES PEOPLE MAKE – A STUDY

❖

A s we made clear in Chapter 2, by studying our mistakes, reflecting on them and discussing them, we can increase the effectiveness of our learning. We identified *fear* as one of the biggest blocks to learning from our mistakes. Owning up to and sharing our mistakes is threatening and can make us feel anxious, which we naturally try to avoid. Mistakes are threatening to us because we see them as negative and associate them with failure. The language we use to describe mistakes is also negative.

We need to find a way of talking about mistakes which reduces the element of threat and fear. A classification or description of the type of mistakes people often make would help us to do this, for we could then discuss mistakes in a 'descriptive' rather than an 'evaluative' way. This was the main reason behind our study; the search for a neutral, descriptive language of mistakes.

THE 'MY BIGGEST MISTAKE' SERIES

We were given a unique opportunity to analyse the mistakes of a number of well-known people in the industrial and political worlds, such as Richard Branson, founder of Virgin, and Anita Roddick, managing director of the Body Shop. There have been several previous studies on mistakes made in laboratories at universities, or using computer simulations at business schools. However, we had access to information on 227 prominent people, describing *in their own words* what they considered to be their biggest real-life mistake.

Between 1989 and 1994 the *Independent on Sunday* ran a series of articles called 'My Biggest Mistake'. The paper made these articles, 227 in all, available to us to analyse. Although there were some limitations to the data, which we discuss later, the opportunity to study the self-described mistakes of well-known senior executives, politicians and entrepreneurs was too good to miss.

The articles provided us with a rare, but very welcome, opportunity. We could extend the work of academic researchers by basing our research on real people, real situations and real mistakes, rather than students and simulations.

THE AIMS OF THE STUDY

We set ourselves two aims at the beginning of the study, which evolved into four as we began to think more deeply around the issues. They were as follows:

O   to generate a classification system leading to a neutral language of mistakes

O   to apply the classification system to real-life mistakes, through the 'My Biggest Mistake' series of articles

O   to analyse the lessons learned by the authors of the articles, and to identify any useful themes or patterns

O   to produce a set of exercises and tools which would help individuals and organizations to self-diagnose the mistakes to which they are most predisposed.

The results of the first two of these aims are described in this chapter. The lessons emerging from the articles are discussed in Chapter 4, and the exercises and tools are described throughout this book.

THE STRENGTHS AND LIMITATIONS OF OUR DATA

The main limitation of our data stems from the fact that the authors were allowed to write the articles themselves (although, paradoxically, this is also a strength). In the research jargon, our data is 'self-reported'. As we will discuss in the next section, the benefits of this particular data set far outweigh the limitations, which are discussed in detail below. The limitations can be grouped under the following headings:

O   Can selective reporting distort the information?

O   Are the mistakes correctly diagnosed?

O   How truthful are the authors?
O   How representative are the authors?
O   How insightful are the authors?

CAN SELECTIVE REPORTING DISTORT THE INFORMATION?

The information we have analysed consists of 227 short descriptions (about 500 words) of mistakes written by the authors themselves. They are self-reported statements and so rely on the memory of the authors. Our memory is not perfect and is subject to a variety of distortions that we may not even be aware of. We may only remember selective facts, for example, or we may reconstruct chaotic and unplanned events with the benefit of hindsight, reporting what appears to be a coherent and planned series of actions. We may even 'remember' things that never happened. It is therefore likely that the articles analysed may contain factual or proce-dural inaccuracies.

ARE THE MISTAKES CORRECTLY DIAGNOSED?

We saw in Chapter 2 how corporate executives tend to remember events that go well and attribute them to their own actions. They also manage to forget events which go badly, or attribute them to other people, or to fac-tors beyond their control. These patterns of interpretation of events are called 'attribution errors'. We are usually not aware that we are making attribution errors and so they are difficult to spot. Again, it is likely that some of the reasons for mistakes reported in the articles may have been incorrectly attributed.

HOW TRUTHFUL ARE THE AUTHORS?

We have discussed in some detail the feelings and emotions which pre-vent people from reflecting on and discussing their mistakes. We can imagine that when you are asked to share your thoughts with the readers of a national Sunday newspaper, your emotions may be felt even more intensely. Many of the authors of the articles are well known to the public, and famous people often have an image which they wish to portray and protect. Add to that the public relations value of the column which gave authors the opportunity to 'advertise their wares', and you have to wonder how truthful people were being about their 'mistakes'. In fact some of the pieces were blatant examples of corporate advertising or self-publicity. Some did not even contain a mistake, merely the 'opinion' of the esteemed contributor. We separated these out into a 'miscellaneous' cate-gory and concentrated on the remainder.

HOW REPRESENTATIVE ARE THE AUTHORS?

Does our sample of 227 authors represent the typical executive/senior politician, or does it represent the newspaper editor's circle of friends? Can we apply, or 'generalize', our results to other business and political leaders, or to other groups of people? In this case, we submit the spread and coverage of industrial sectors and job titles associated with the authors as evidence of a widely representative sample. The number of people in the sample, 227, is also quite large for this type of study and so it is more likely to provide generally applicable results.

HOW INSIGHTFUL ARE THE AUTHORS?

As Abigail Sellen has pointed out, the 'empirical evidence suggests that some errors are more easily detected than others'.[1] It should therefore be expected that some mistakes may be under-reported, simply because they are less obvious to the author. A lack of *insight* may therefore reduce the reporting of some types of mistakes. Similarly, other mistakes may be easy to spot, for example not monitoring or checking facts will usually have a clear outcome which is difficult to miss. Mistakes such as these may be over-reported. The relative frequency of different types of mistakes is interesting, yet not a vital piece of information. The fact that a mistake occurs with any degree of frequency is perhaps more important for our purposes.

THE STRENGTHS OF OUR SAMPLE

The limitations of our data apply to all studies dealing with real-life events – indeed the more practical and realistic (and therefore useful) the study, the more difficulties there are likely to be associated with it. Nevertheless it was important that we took the limitations of our data into account when we analysed them. We have therefore endeavoured not to over-interpret our findings and not to use high-level statistical analysis, which would be inappropriate in this situation.

This sample does, however, have many advantages. It is always interesting to listen to prominent and successful people, but 227 of them describing in their own words what they considered to be their 'biggest mistake' and, more importantly, what they learned from it, provides a unique opportunity for us to learn from their collective experience. Even allowing for the likely biases and distortions outlined above (which led us to drop about 10 per cent of the articles), they represent a unique set of self-described experiences. The research that has been carried out in this area has been largely based on simulations in the form of business games or computer simulations. Our sample is not based on students or managers from business schools and we did not gather our data from a laboratory. This would certainly have been more convenient and easier to control, but would have been further away from the real world. Our authors provide information from a wide range of industries, job types and nations. We feel their mistakes are representative of the types commonly made in business and politics.

There are other strong reasons for carrying out the study. We have reviewed the importance of learning, both within and outside of the workplace, and we have indicated the important role mistakes can take in the learning process. The need for a neutral language with which to discuss mistakes is great, as is the need for self-diagnostic tools to help us identify our common mistakes. This research has provided both.

A DESCRIPTION OF OUR SAMPLE

We were provided with 227 usable articles from the *Independent on Sunday*. The authors had an average age of 50 years, the oldest being 72 and the youngest 28 (63 did not report their age). Only 10 per cent of the authors were women, reflecting their under-representation among senior-level jobs. In terms of job title *at the time of writing* (as opposed to at the time of the mistake), most authors held a board-level or senior executive-level position. Table 3.1 shows the breakdown of job titles within our sample.

TABLE 3.1   Job titles of authors

Job title	%
Chairman	19
Chief executive/CEO	10
Chairman and CE/CEO	4
Managing director	18
Functional director	4
Founder	14
Combinations of chairman, MD, founder and functional director	5
Other (e.g. politicians, union members, academics)	15
Not stated	11

TABLE 3.2 Authors' area of employment

Employment sector	%
Miscellaneous	13
PR/advertising/marketing	11
Finance	10
Government/employer organizations	9
Heavy engineering/energy	8
Retail	7
Entertainment	6
Hotel/restaurants/leisure	6
Consulting/training	6
Publishing	5
IT/telecommunications	5
Transport/distribution	4
Consumer goods manufacture	4
Design	3
Academia	3

At the time of writing their articles, the authors worked in a range of industrial sectors and markets, from finance to consumer goods manufacture, to advertising, government and academia. A breakdown of these appears in Table 3.2.

Of the 169 who reported their nationality, the majority (143, or 85%) were from the UK or Ireland, and 15 (9%) were from North America, with the remainder hailing from the rest of Europe or elsewhere.

The authors therefore represent a wide range of top-level positions in a wide range of organizations and areas of work. In terms of gender and nationality they are less diverse, being, on the whole, men from the UK.

WHEN AND WHERE DID THE MISTAKES OCCUR?

All mistakes occur in some kind of context. We wanted to discover whether we are more likely to make a particular kind of mistake in a particular situation or context. To do this we first needed to analyse the contexts in which the mistakes made by our authors occurred.

The process we used for analysing the articles was as follows:

1   We three authors took the same 25 randomly selected articles and
      identified the themes that emerged. These included both mistakes
      and the contexts in which they occurred.
2   The themes were discussed, refined and compared, first with
      Senge's seven learning disabilities,[2] and then with Dörner and
      Schaub's taxonomy.
3   A new taxonomy was devised, combining the Dörner and Schaub
      taxonomy and our own experience. This was then applied to all
      230 articles. Three articles were rejected as we did not feel that
      they contained mistakes. The second and third authors then took
      half each of the remaining articles but both coded every tenth arti-
      cle as a reliability check.
4   The authors then discussed their coding, compared the articles in
      common, and discussed problem articles. The classification was
      revised for a final time.
5   Each article was then recoded for a final time, by the second and
      third authors (who took half each).

We identified five broad contexts in which mistakes were made:

O   relationships with people
O   managing an organization
O   personal choice
O   cultural differences
O   miscellaneous.

Figure 3.1 shows the overall proportions of mistakes which fell into each
of these categories.

    We broke down two of these categories, 'relationships with people' and
'managing an organization', into more specific contexts. The full classification is described in Table 3.3.

    The proportions of mistakes that fell into each category are shown in
Table 3.4.

MANAGING AN ORGANIZATION

The greatest number of mistakes occurred when our authors were managing their organizations. This rather broad term includes tasks carried out at
all levels of management.

    For example, 33 per cent of the mistakes occurred at high-level man-
agement, such as making strategic decisions as to the direction of the
business, bringing about change in terms of the structure or culture of the

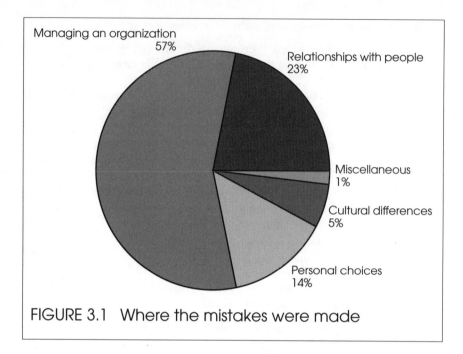

Managing an organization
57%

Relationships with people
23%

Miscellaneous
1%

Cultural differences
5%

Personal choices
14%

FIGURE 3.1   Where the mistakes were made

organization, or managing the expansion of business. Sir Adam Thomson's decision to buy BAC 1–11 aeroplanes for British Caledonian, rather than Boeing 737s, is an example of a mistake at the strategic level. The mistakes reported by Anthony Cleaver when trying to make IBM UK Holdings more customer focused is an example of a mistake in the context of managing change. Finally, the mistakes made by Sophie Mirman and Janet Reger fall firmly into the context of managing business expansion.

Nine per cent of the mistakes were made when developing or launching a new product, such as George Bull, chairman of IDV, when relaunching J&B Whisky. Finally, 15 per cent of the mistakes occurred during day-to-day operations. For example, Eric Thornton mistakenly ordering 5,760 pairs of tights instead of 240, or Brian Taylor, chief executive of Wardley Stores, ordering fifteen tons of the wrong size of fish.

RELATIONSHIPS WITH PEOPLE

Many of the mistakes occurred when the authors were dealing with people. These included mistakes made when managing a partnership

TABLE 3.3   Where the mistakes were made

RELATIONSHIPS WITH PEOPLE

Business relationships and partnerships
Dealings with people in the context of forming and maintaining partnerships where the issue is one of trust, mutual understanding, compatibility etc.
Relationships with people at work
Managing as well as in contact with.
Customer/supplier relationships
Any situation involving customers or suppliers of any kind, both internal or external, direct or indirect.

MANAGING AN ORGANIZATION

Business expansion
Focus on the non-people side, e.g. financing growth, choosing new markets etc.
Bringing about change
Issues to do with culture and style change, restructuring, redundancies etc.
Strategic choice
Key decisions with long-term implications which are difficult to predict, but which are not purely financial issues.
Operational matters
Anything to do with day-to-day planning, organizing, prioritizing, use of time and resources and routine decisions.
Product development
Developing and/or bringing to market a new product or service.

PERSONAL CHOICE

Anything to do with life choices, personal campaigns; include acting in a pioneering and reforming role.

CULTURAL DIFFERENCES

Anything to do with intercultural and international differences.

MISCELLANEOUS

Mistakes that cannot be classified elsewhere.

---

agreement, such as William Sargent, chairman of Spitting Image Productions and MD of Viva Pictures, 'trying to do business on the strength of a handshake'. Five per cent of mistakes occurred in this context. Eight per cent of mistakes occurred when dealing with people on a day-to-day basis at work, for example Terence Conran's appointment decision for the chief executive of Storehouse, or Lynn Franks the public relations adviser's

TABLE 3.4 Full breakdown of mistakes per context

CONTEXTS	MISTAKES (%)
Relationships with people	
Business relationships and partnerships	5
Relationships with people at work	8
Customer/supplier relationships	10
Managing an organization	
Business expansion	14
Bringing about change	9
Strategic choice	10
Operational matters	15
Product development	9
Personal choice	14
Cultural differences	5
Miscellaneous	1

reluctance to trust and delegate anything to her staff. Finally, 10 per cent of the mistakes occurred when dealing with a customer (in the full sense of the word), or supplier. Examples here are Anita Roddick's experience of not taking into account what her customers wanted when commissioning an advertisement for a charity, and Geraldine Laybourne's decision not to consult the customers of her intended children's programme (i.e. the children).

PERSONAL CHOICES AND REGRETS

Nearly 14 per cent of mistakes the authors made were in the context of what we termed 'personal choice'. Many concerned decisions over career moves – such as Lady Anson who regretted not attending Oxford or Cambridge University, and John Bintliff, chairman of Elan, who regretted staying in the public sector too long. Other examples were Sir Peter Parker, chairman of British Rail from 1976–1983, and his decision not to take French citizenship, and Norman Willis's choice not to take up the cause of women's representation in the trades union movement early enough.

CULTURAL DIFFERENCES

Finally, 5 per cent of the mistakes occurred when working across cultures. Prime examples came from Alan Capper, chairman of Rowland Worldwide public relations consultancy, who underestimated the difficulties of trying to arrange a photoshoot in Moscow for Andrew Lloyd Webber, and from Gerry Cottle, whose ill-fated circus trip to Iran cost him dear.

Exercise 3.1 (p.74) helps you to identify the context in which you are most likely to make a mistake.

CLASSIFYING THE MISTAKES

We classified the mistakes our authors made into several broad categories. The percentages are shown in Figure 3.2.

Again, we broke down these broad categories into more specific mistakes. The full classification scheme is shown in Table 3.5.

The proportions of each of these types of mistakes which occurred are shown in Table 3.6.

SETTING GOALS – DEFINING GOALS AND PURPOSE

If we don't know where we are going, we are unlikely to get there. This ancient piece of folklore seems intuitively to be true. There is also a large

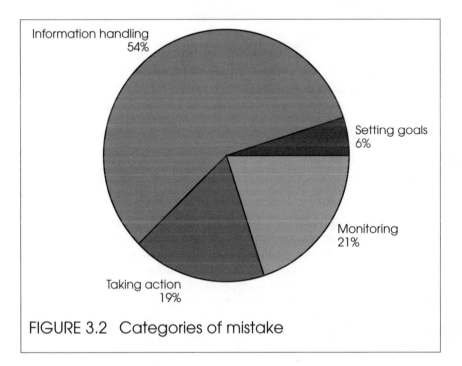

FIGURE 3.2 Categories of mistake

TABLE 3.5   Kinds of mistakes made

SETTING GOALS

Defining goals and purpose
Working with unclear or competing goals, or not agreeing goals with others.

INFORMATION HANDLING

Entrenchment
Being overwhelmed by amount of information, and as a result unable to act or decide.
Generalizing
Planning and working on the basis of assumptions and generalizations that are not tested.
Selectivity
Concentrating on only a narrow or small part of the available or potentially available information; ignoring potentially useful information.
Blinkered thinking
Acting without regard for consequences or side-effects; more concerned with the present.

TAKING ACTION

Pressure to act
Acting quickly in response to internal or external pressures.
Over-rationalizing
Refusing to act on the basis of gut feel/intuition.

MONITORING

Monitoring what is happening
Assuming that things are happening, or will happen, without the need to check or ensure that they are happening.
Self-reflecting
Not reflecting on actions taken, or considering underlying causes of failure or success.

---

amount of scientific evidence to support it. Researchers working in the area of 'goal-setting theory' argue that setting realistic, yet achievable, goals helps us to become motivated to achieve them. Research also shows that those of us who work to specific, yet stretching, goals perform better, both in the work setting and in our personal achievements. At work many organizations make use of formal performance management systems, most of which include some element of objective or goal setting. At home it is also vital to set ourselves clear goals: 'where we want to be' in a year's time; when we want to buy our first house or new car, for example. With-

TABLE 3.6 Proportions of mistakes made

MISTAKE	%
Setting goals	
Defining goals and purpose	6
Information handling	
Entrenchment	1
Generalizing	27
Selectivity	14
Blinkered thinking	12
Taking action	
Pressure to act	9
Over-rationalizing	10
Monitoring	
Monitoring what is happening	16
Self-reflecting	5

out goals we soon find that another year has slipped by without any great achievements.

Many mistakes can therefore emerge as a result of the goal-setting process. We have found in our own work with client organizations that when learning a complex task, successful groups spend nearly twice as long as unsuccessful groups in the preparation phase, discussing the purpose of the exercise and setting themselves clear tasks. This pattern was also found by Dörner and Schaub[3] when they compared experienced managers with students taking part in a business game. Common mistakes in this area can include not balancing conflicting goals, not setting clear goals, or setting inappropriate goals. Of the mistakes described by the authors 6 per cent were explained by the lack of clear goals. George Walker, the former boxer and ex-chief executive of Brent Walker, the leisure and brewing company, described his ordeal in 1982 when struggling to save his company:

> My biggest mistake was staking my home life against my business life and nearly losing both . . . Eventually I borrowed £2.7 million from a small independent bank in Brighton called TCB, at an interest rate of 4 per cent over Libor. I guaranteed the loan personally, putting up all my properties, including my home, against it . . . If the company went down, we would be penniless.

Not managing to balance conflicting goals occurs most often when we are working in complex environments, where goals may not all be achievable, or where some prioritization is necessary. George Walker had two goals:

to keep his business afloat, and to keep his home and family together. He failed to keep these two goals separate, and to balance them. As he says:

> At the end of it, I realised that the real mistake was subjecting my wife and family to that. I would never again stake my home and family against a business. If I want to put my neck on the block or commit business suicide, that's fine, but I won't drag my wife and family down with me.

Another example is from Paul Southgate, chief executive of Wickens Tutt Southgate, the design consultancy. At a time when his business was just beginning to take off, he also committed himself to writing a book, for delivery in six months. Two years and six months later he completed it on the plane to Sydney en route to his own wedding!

INFORMATION HANDLING

In our study, the largest proportion of mistakes – 54 per cent – was associated with handling information. This should not be surprising. We live in an age where knowledge is power and the amount of information available to us is immense. We cannot cope with such overload and our brains often act to simplify matters for us. It is this process of simplification which leads to so many of the mistakes that we make. Unfortunately the process of filtering and simplifying the information we have to work with is largely unconscious and if we are not wise to the possibility of it happening then we may not even notice until it is too late. We identified four types of mistake that are connected to the way we handle information, and these are discussed below.

ENTRENCHMENT

Entrenchment as a phenomenon was observed by *Dörner* and Schaub in their series of experiments:

> Sometimes [people] become entrenched in information collection. They feel uncertain and not ready to act, so they try to get more information as a basis for decision-making. Bewildered by the new facets of the problem provided by new information, they decide that still more information is necessary. The new information, again, convinces them even more that the information at their disposal is not at all sufficient. And so on ad infinitum.

We can probably all recall a time when after poring over a mass of information, we are still no nearer to making any sense of it. That feeling of a loss of control, accompanied by rising panic, may have been familiar to

Richard Simpson, chief executive of Price's Patent Candle Company. A successful career in the city was brought to a premature end when he acquired the company as a hobby, but without telling his employers. In his words:

> I had nowhere to go but into the business I had just acquired. On my first morning I arrived at this large empty desk in a large and equally empty office and wondered what on earth I was supposed to do.

In summary, we experience entrenchment when we are overloaded with information and cannot decide what to do. The end result is that we do nothing.

GENERALIZING

By far the largest number of mistakes made (27 per cent) fell into this category. We defined it earlier as the result of 'planning and working on the basis of assumptions and generalizations that are not tested'. But what does this mean?

In Chapter 2 we discussed the concept of mindsets, or mental models, and how they can influence our behaviour without us being aware of this fact. Consider, for example, the shape of the motor car in the UK before Ford launched the Sierra model. Cars were boxy, flat and angular. Then, suddenly, the Sierra appeared. This car was rounded, smooth and curvy. The car took a while to gain acceptance; it did not fit with our mental model of what a car should be. Many motor manufacturers dismissed this design, using words such as 'It'll never catch on.' They acted on an untested generalization of the type: 'People won't like that type of design, they won't buy it, the future of car design is angular.' They were wrong. The Sierra changed the way we think about cars – it changed our mental model. The result? The vast majority of cars produced today owe a great deal to the design of the Sierra, and square boxy cars are a thing of the past.

Peter Webber, managing director of My Kinda Town, the international restaurant group including Chicago Rib Shack, Henry J Beans, and Chicago Meatpackers, gave an example of a mistake he made involving generalization. Webber describes the background to the mistake:

> I first met Bob Payton in 1980, by which time he'd already had huge success in London with his Chicago Pizza Pie Factory. Two years later, we were having lunch together and he told me he was going to take over a Bejam freezer centre in a side street near Harrods, and turn it into a barbecue restaurant. He said he would call it the Chicago Rib Shack, and the only things on the menu would be a rack of ribs and a loaf of fried onions. He asked me to go into partnership with him.

The mistake he made was this:

> I thought he was off his rocker . . . I couldn't imagine people eating ribs with their fingers. And how could you offer a menu of just two items? The project was already funded through venture capitalists. All he wanted me to do was work the restaurant with him and share the profits . . . I just couldn't see how this would work, so I said no.

Peter Webber had a model, or image, of what a restaurant should be. The model did not look anything like the proposed Rib Shack and so he decided not to become involved. He was guided by an untested assumption that people would not go to such a restaurant. However, he soon regretted the decision:

> Within six months . . . [1983], the Chicago Rib Shack had 8,000 customers a week paying about £12 a head. By 1987 it was making more than £1 million profit. Restaurants just don't make money like that.

A similar example is given by the managing director of Hasbro UK, the toy company. His biggest mistake was turning down the opportunity to bid for the rights to the Teenage Mutant Ninja Turtles. For those of you who missed out on this phenomenon, the turtles were immensely popular children's cartoon characters who spent their time fighting 'baddies' and eating pizza. There were also a number of successful feature films and other products associated with them.

> The mistake was taking a middle-aged adult view of the world. Children are fascinated by the battle between good and evil, and it never goes away. And the Turtles were wacky and modern (they craved pizza), which appealed to the rebellious side of children.

Again the mistake was in taking his model of 'what is interesting', and applying it to children without checking the assumption. The need for making explicit our models and 'testing' them is clearly important.

SELECTIVITY

Often when there is a wide variety of information available to us we focus on one small part of what is available. For example, we know from studies of interviews used for recruitment that the interviewers remember and attach more importance to negative information about the job candidate than to positive information. We also know that how we feel about something or someone affects the way we handle information about them. For example, one study asked two sets of opposing football fans to watch a video of the two teams playing each other. Afterwards each set of fans could remember the good things that their side had done, and the foul play of the other side, but not vice-versa. We can see that our mental models direct us to focus on certain aspects of the available information ('my team is a fair team, and does not engage in foul play'). Mistakes of *selectivity* are therefore closely related to those of *generalization.*

Mistakes of a selective nature made up 14 per cent of our sample. A clear example comes from Sam Wauchope, managing director of Acorn, the computer manufacturers. His biggest mistake was 'allowing the debts of one of our distributors to get out of control'. Acorn were pushing for growth. They had used this distributor for several years and Acorn were their biggest supplier.

> The first sign that all was not well was when we began to get slight delays in payments. What used to be a monthly payment was now split into two, three or even four, with the odd little excuses here and there.
>
> . . . I should have been more cautious. However, as the new MD, I was so determined Acorn was going to grow that *I only heard what I wanted to hear.* I accepted it was a temporary blip, that the market had been slow for a month or two, but that things were looking up.

Wauchope was in a new job. Times were exciting and he had a lot to think about. He wanted the distributor to succeed, and his model of them was as a successful company. He therefore ignored any information that did not fit this model. The consequences were as follows:

> When our distributors finally went out of business, we were forced to pick up the tab. There was a total loss of around £1 million, which for a company of Acorn's size was no small loss.

Another example of this type of mistake came from Paul Layzell, director of Leadership Dynamics Europe, and ex-managing director of one of BMW's import subsidiaries.

> Because we were a top-performing company with spectacular growth in sales and profitability from marketing and distributing a prestigious product, I didn't question our management processes earlier. I should have.

Layzell was blinded to the need for change because of the bottom-line success the organization was achieving. This is a good example of success hampering learning and development. With the company doing so well, there was no apparent need to change, and so they did not. Of course, the economic environment changes rapidly and what works well today may not work well tomorrow. Success fosters complacency and reduces the motivation to experiment and innovate, which in the long term is a mistake. Layzell eventually realized his mistake after a chance meeting with Ralph Stayer, owner of another business in the US, but the story illustrates one of the disadvantages of short-term success.

BLINKERED THINKING

Jay Forrester, Peter Senge and colleagues at MIT have made a great contribution to our understanding of how organizations work through the introduction of 'system dynamics' and systems thinking. The fundamental belief underlying their approach is that organizations (of all kinds) are integrated and so no one person can act without affecting the whole system. There is a strong interrelationship between the design function, production, marketing and finance in a computer manufacturing company, for example. Decisions taken by a manager in the finance function will have an impact on how another manager works in the marketing function, say. Furthermore, what is best for finance may not be best for marketing, or *for the organization as a whole*. The same principle holds true for government bodies, charitable ventures, and any organization of people. We have to learn that our decisions and action will have an impact on the work of others *now*, and *in the future*, and the discipline of systems thinking aims to help us learn about this process.

However, systems thinking widely 'hurts'. As we have said, our capacity for processing information is limited and as a consequence of this our brains tend to simplify things. For this reason many of the errors we make tend to be because we are thinking too narrowly – blinkered thinking – and failing to take into account the consequences or side-effects of our actions, both in the present and in the future.

Of the mistakes described by the 'My Biggest Mistake' authors 12 per cent were attributed to 'blinkered thinking'. The following example illustrates it in terms of the future effects of actions. Janet Reger was chairman of Designs by Janet Reger, the lingerie and swimwear designer. She was running a successful business from a small premises near Bond Street in London. She decided to move to a more prestigious location in Bond Street, even though the rent would be £25,000 a year, as compared to her then current rent of £7,000. She describes what happened next:

> Bond Street being Bond Street, we wanted to make the shop look wonderfully elegant, so for the first time in our lives we started doing things we couldn't afford to do.
>
> Up until then we'd always borrowed small sums which we were able to pay back in two or three years. But Bond Street took us into a new realm of borrowing. Instead of being able to pay it back quite easily, we were beginning to rely on high projections.

Reger took on a financial commitment without fully exploring its impact on other areas of the business, for example cash flow. She also did not allow for future possibilities, such as interest rate rises and rent increases. In the end a combination of stagnant turnover, taking on more financial burdens and increases in rent and interest rates forced the company to fold.

> We were having to pay out more and more, but our turnover wasn't increasing, because of recession. That was the beginning of our troubles. We tried various ways of increasing our turnover, but they all cost more money . . . If we had stayed in low rent accommodation, I have no doubt we would have survived.

Another example of blinkered thinking is offered by David James, ex-managing director at various Rank Organisation subsidiaries. He was asked to take over as managing director of English Numbering Machines (ENM), a troubled subsidiary of Rank.

> By January 1977, ENM was recording serious losses. The market for its traditional products had shrunk, while its later developments were effectively only sub-components that went into other companies' products . . . ENM was over dependent on somebody else's marketing success to keep running a factory which had more than its share of problems.

To turn the company around, James embarked on a £2 million modernization of the factory in order to cut production overheads drastically and to create greater production flexibility. This was completed in 18 months, but to no avail, and eventually the factory had to be closed down and the company sold. What went wrong?

> The problem was that however advanced the new production facilities might be, they were still useless unless there was an actual demand for what it had to offer. It had been a wrong decision to restructure ENM's production operations in the absence of any obvious solution to this problem.

James had acted to solve a problem (possibly on the basis of his mental model of what a solution to a large business problem should be) without looking at the effects (or lack of them) of his solution on the real problem. He had acted without considering the wider system in which his organization operated.

TAKING ACTION

Once we have analysed the information available to us, worked out the pros and cons, costs and benefits, and implications of our ideas, we have to put them into action. Nineteen per cent of the mistakes made by the authors occurred at this stage, and they fell into two categories: 'Pressure to act' (acting quickly in response to internal or external pressures) and 'Over-rationalizing' (refusing to act on the basis of gut feel/intuition).

PRESSURE TO ACT

Have you ever thought that if only you had more time, you could produce a perfect piece of work? If it wasn't for all those customers constantly interrupting you, or your manager piling the pressure on by moving your deadlines, you know you could really deliver a quality job. However, we rarely have the luxury of operating in a relaxed environment. Of the mistakes made by our authors 9 per cent were caused by acting rashly when under pressure. Even if there is no pressure from external sources, we may apply our own 'internal' pressure, for example by being too eager to clinch that deal, or acting on impulse.

An amusing yet potentially serious example of making a mistake due to 'internal' pressure was given by John Willan, managing director of the London Philharmonic Orchestra. He began his career as an assistant at EMI's Abbey Road studios and on one particular occasion was coordinating the tea breaks between the London Philharmonic in one studio and a big band in another. This involved running up and down stairs to liaise with the assistant engineer:

> There was a bit of banter building up, and at one point I tore upstairs and dashed into the studio, failing to notice that the red light was on and they were recording. I got some friendly abuse from Alan [the assistant engineer], and in response, I made to stab at the stop button on this huge 24-track machine to give him a fright. The trouble was I actually hit the button . . . I just died.

As it turned out, the producer of the session saw the funny side:

> Somehow I managed to keep my job, but it taught me quite a lesson. When you're working, you do not mess about . . . You have to think before you leap.

Examples on a larger scale of acting on the basis of internal pressure came from Sir John Harvey-Jones, who kept ICI in the oil business for too long because of his love for oil exploration, and David Woods, managing director of Scottish Provident, who when trying to change the culture of the organization 'made the mistake of losing patience with my company and trying to rush it'.

Hollywood film director Franc Roddam gave a clear example of a mistake he made due to pressure imposed by an external source, in this case the film star Robert Redford. After spending six months in the Amazon writing a script about the rain forest:

> . . . the result was so good that Robert Redford was interested. Then having initially said he wanted to do it, everything went quiet . . . By this time, [he] was three weeks and 11 hours late for a meeting. I kept getting calls saying things like: 'He's on the way – he is on the motorway now.

He's driving up from Salt Lake City.' So by the time he arrived, I was angry.

Roddam was frustrated and he let the pressure get to him and influence his actions. This was his mistake.

I said: 'I have been waiting for more than seven months for you to say yes or no on this film . . . I want your answer, and I'm giving you exactly one week.' Ten days later, he turned it down . . . The studio lost interest.

OVER-RATIONALIZING

We have noted that sometimes we make mistakes when we act too quickly on the basis of impulse or pressure. Sometimes there are circumstances, however, where acting on the basis of a hunch, or 'gut feel', may be entirely appropriate. Indeed, 10 per cent of the mistakes made in our sample were because the authors did not act on the basis of their intuition.

As Henry Drnec, chief executive officer of Maison Caurette, the beer distributor, said:

If you know your business well enough, you ought to be willing to take a chance on a product that you believe in.

Drnec was a senior director of marketing at Gallo, the largest producer of wine in the world. In an attempt to increase the volume of wine drunk in bars and pubs, he set out to create a wine-based drink, such as a wine-soda mix.

We took it to our in-house market research department, which set up focus groups in nine cities over 14 days at a cost of more than $100,000. I went to every single one, and I can't tell you how much people hated our product . . . After two weeks on the road, I came home absolutely hammered saying that . . . it was a complete failure and we shouldn't do it.

Drnec had an idea which made sense to him. He knew his industry better than most, but the market research told him he was wrong. His biggest mistake was to allow this research to dictate a big decision and not to trust his own judgement, because:

At the same time 100 miles away there were two guys making a product in their garage called California Cooler. Four years later they sold out to Brown Foreman, a big US distiller, for £150 million, and the 'wine cooler' became a phenomenon.

John Hougham, chairman of ACAS, the advisory, conciliation and arbitration service in the UK, and ex-director of industrial relations for Ford of

Europe, found that his first impulse turned out to be true – that the employee involvement scheme that had been successful in the US would not work in the UK. Unfortunately, he allowed himself to be persuaded otherwise. Debbie Moore of Pineapple Limited, the dance and fashion business, wanted to run a manual inventory and invoicing system until her new computerized version had proved itself. She was persuaded against this by the 'experts' – an unfortunate piece of advice which cost her over £100,000.

MONITORING

Monitoring our work has become increasingly important over the last few years. This is partly because the need for high-quality products and services has grown. Failing to monitor our actions and their effects can be a big mistake. We will draw a distinction between mistakes caused by a lack of *monitoring,* i.e. those which involve assuming that things are happening, or will happen, without checking, and those caused by a lack of reflection, which involve a failure to think back on actions taken, or to consider the underlying causes of our mistakes or successes. Of the mistakes we found 21 per cent involved errors associated with not monitoring or reflecting.

MONITORING WHAT IS HAPPENING

Norman Adsetts, Chairman of Sheffield Insulations Group, made a big mistake during wartime when he was in the Royal Air Force. He lost an aeroplane.

> It was my responsibility to keep records of everything in stock at a large flying school. One day we were preparing . . . for a visit by the Air Ministry auditors. I still remember the moment when they walked into my office and asked: 'Flying Officer Adsetts, what about this aeroplane?' 'What aeroplane?' I responded. Then they asked me a straightforward and fairly obvious question. 'Where is it?'

Luckily the plane turned up and Adsetts was let off the hook. He assumed that the system designed to monitor the movement of aeroplanes was working and so did not bother to check it. This nearly proved costly – if it hadn't been found, he might still be paying for it.

Even more embarrassing was the failure of Michael Day, chairman of the Huge Cheese Company, to find out what the Dutch Prime Minister Ruud Lubbers looked like before he met him.

> Eventually, someone came and took us upstairs. He led us into a spectacular octagonal room overlooking a small lake, and we chatted over a cup

of coffee . . . Assuming that he was Ruud Lubbers's secretary, I gave him some cheese as a backhander and asked him to see that the Prime Minister was given the rest. At this point my girlfriend said 'This is the Prime Minister.'

Checking details can be a great effort, yet not doing so is a big mistake which can lead to some unfortunate situations. Of the mistakes made by our authors 16 per cent resulted from them not monitoring their situation.

SELF-REFLECTING

Making mistakes is all very well, but mistakes on their own will not tell us anything. The value of a mistake lies in the lessons we learn from it, not in the mistake itself. (This theme is taken up again in Chapter 4.) We cannot hope to learn from our mistakes unless we stop, take time out, and simply think the mistake through. What did I do? Why did I do it? What did this or that action lead to? The process of going back over our mistakes in this way is known as reflecting, and failing to reflect on our actions may be the greatest mistake of all. Without reflecting, we cannot learn from our mistakes.

Of course, as we have discussed, the process of reflecting on our mistakes can be uncomfortable, threatening and anxiety-provoking. Small wonder that failing to reflect is a common mistake. Indeed, 5 per cent of the mistakes we found were in this category.

TWO INSIGHTS FROM OUR ANALYSIS OF MISTAKES

The authors of the newspaper series certainly made some large and colourful mistakes. Some are undoubtedly entertaining in their own right. They also serve to highlight some important points about the mistakes commonly made by people in their everyday lives. Two themes emerged from our analysis:

O   the importance of information handling
O   the cyclic nature of mistakes.

THE IMPORTANCE OF INFORMATION HANDLING

The largest set of mistakes (54 per cent) were related to information handling. This should not be surprising. We have noted that a defining part of people's lives at the end of the 1990s is the ever-increasing amount of information we have to deal with. At work management information systems ensure that any and every business performance measure can quickly be made available. Informal networks and systems also conspire to bring more facts and figures our way. At home we are bombarded with information through the mass media. The Internet now potentially offers us access to almost any information we could want. However, the majority of these data flying at us are useless. Most of the information we come across is irrelevant to our needs. Picking our way through the dross, and through interesting but misleading information, simply results in confusion and overload. We cannot cope. Whilst the information age is supposed to offer us choice and freedom, in fact it offers us paralysis, indecision and parochialism. Our brains process information and one of the best tricks we have learned is how to filter out the irrelevant and concentrate on the useful. This is becoming increasingly difficult.

As our brains take more and more shortcuts to help us cope, we make more and more mistakes. We make decisions based on only a small part of the available information; perhaps information which is familiar to us, or which conforms to our stereotypes. We may proceed on the basis of assumptions or generalizations which are not fully explored, or even re-cognized. We may decide on a course of action without fully appreciating the effects that action will have on other people or systems, either now or in the future. Finally, we may even decide not to make a decision at all until we can get more information, which in turn leads us to the search for more information, and so on. Clearly these mistakes are difficult to spot and careful reflection is necessary to identify the mental shortcuts we have taken, and may take again, that led to the mistake. The tools and exercises described throughout this book are designed to help you do just that.

THE CYCLE OF MISTAKES

Using the classification scheme developed above, we can see our actions fitting into a cycle (see Figure 3.3).

Any action should begin with the setting of a goal or goals. Where are we going to direct our efforts? We then need to handle information to decide what we are going to do, how exactly, and when. We then take the action and finally monitor the effects and success of it, hopefully learning through this final purpose so that when we set our next goal we will be even more successful!

Reflecting back on the different kinds of mistakes we found from our research, we can see a clear parallel. Different kinds of mistakes relate to different stages of the action cycle (see Figure 3.4).

Use Exercise 3.2 (p.76) to help you think about where in the cycle your mistakes are more likely to occur.

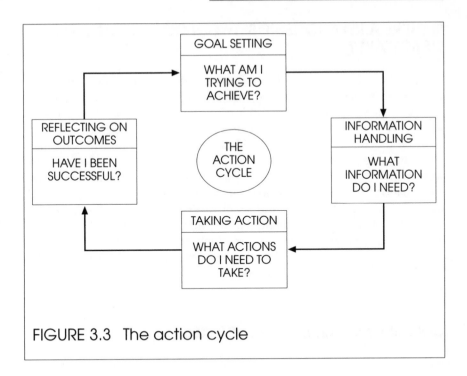

FIGURE 3.3   The action cycle

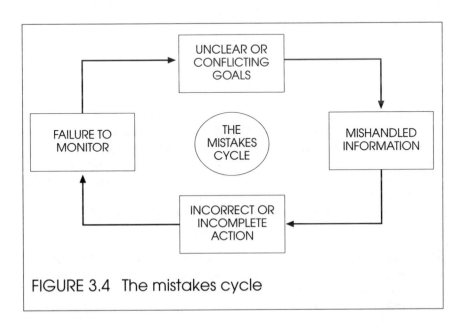

FIGURE 3.4   The mistakes cycle

IS THERE A RELATIONSHIP BETWEEN CONTEXT AND TYPE OF MISTAKE?

Having classified and counted the mistakes described in the articles, the contexts in which they occurred, the industrial sectors they occurred in and the demographic characteristics of the authors, our next step was to see if any relationships existed between these. For example, are certain contexts or situations associated with a particular mistake? Are some mistakes more common in certain industrial sectors than in others? Do women make the same types of mistakes as men? We looked at all the combinations that our data would allow, including combinations of mistakes with age and job title, and in all cases found *no clear relationship*. We thus feel confident in saying that the mistakes we have identified are indiscriminate; people of all ages, positions, and industries can make similar mistakes. We are all vulnerable and can all benefit from taking a closer look at the mistakes we make.

CLASSIFYING YOUR OWN MISTAKES

We set out to produce a classification system and a neutral language with which to talk about the mistakes we commonly make, and to apply that system to the articles in the *Independent on Sunday's* 'My Biggest Mistake' series.

We identified nine common mistakes. The first concerned the setting and defining of goals and objectives. Four mistakes involved difficulty with information handling: focusing selectively on a small part of the information available; becoming overloaded with too much information; acting on the basis of untested assumptions and generalizations, and planning without giving thought to the wider implications of decisions. Two common mistakes were identified involving the taking of action: acting under pressure, and failing to listen to one's instincts and gut feel. Finally, there were mistakes where people failed to check or monitor progress, and where they did not reflect on their behaviour, hence missing the opportunity to learn.

If you want to see the types of mistakes you are most prone to make, try Exercise 3.2 (p.76).

This chapter has described the research we carried out to analyse the mistakes of a number of well-known people in the industrial and political worlds, as published in the 'My Biggest Mistake' series of articles in the *Independent on Sunday*. We discussed the limitations of this data, noting that the benefits far outweigh these limitations. We have described our findings – where the mistakes were made and the types of mistakes made – and illustrated our classification system with real examples from our study. We have also designed two exercises to help you identify where you are most likely to make mistakes and the kinds of mistakes you tend to make.

REFERENCES

1 Sellen, A.J. (1994), 'Detection of everyday errors', *International Review of Applied Psychology*, 43, 4, pp.475–498.
2 Senge, P. (1990), *The Fifth Discipline: The art and practice of the learning organisation*, New York: Doubleday.
3 Dörner, D. and Schaub, H. (1994), 'Errors in planning and decision-making and the nature of human information-processing', *Applied Psychology: An International Review*, 43, 4.

EXERCISE 3.1 WHERE AM I MOST LIKELY TO MAKE MISTAKES?

On balance where do you think you are most likely to make your bigger mistakes? Distribute 10 points across the four categories. Make sure the four numbers add up to ten.

Relationships with people

Managing an organization or complex events

Personal choices

Cross-cultural differences

Total =

Would your close friends or colleagues agree? If in doubt, check.

Now write down as many as you can remember of the more important mistakes that you have made in the past, including the recurring ones. Refer to Exercise 1.1 (p.17) and Exercise 2.2 (p.40).

Read through the descriptions and then rate yourself on the items below. Think about your mistakes in the light of the statements below, and reflect on whether they have occurred in these situations.

RELATIONSHIPS

	MY MISTAKES HAVE OCCURRED IN THIS SITUATION		
Forming and maintaining relationships with people, especially where trust, mutual understanding and compatibility are important	YES	?	NO
Relationships with people at work in general	YES	?	NO
Relationships with people I manage	YES	?	NO
Relationships with people in other organizations who I have dealings with in the course of my work	YES	?	NO

MANAGING AND COPING

Day-to-day planning, organizing, prioritizing, use of time	YES	?	NO
Bringing about change (improvements, reorganization etc.)	YES	?	NO

Managing growth and expansion	YES	?	NO
Introducing new products, processes, ideas etc.	YES	?	NO
Making strategic and longer-term decisions	YES	?	NO

PERSONAL CHOICES

Choices you have made in your life which you made for wrong reasons	YES	?	NO
Regrets (you made the choice for good reasons at the time but subsequently wished you hadn't)	YES	?	NO
Things you always wanted to do but did not	YES	?	NO

CULTURAL DIFFERENCES

Things that you did (or did not do) that were not appropriate given the cultural beliefs and behaviour of another group	YES	?	NO

To confirm your analysis, ask a colleague or friend to fill it in about you. Then ask for their supporting evidence.

What does this analysis tell you?

EXERCISE 3.2   WHAT TYPE OF MISTAKES DO I TEND TO MAKE?

WHERE in the action cycle are you most likely to make mistakes? Shade in up to ten bars in each section, but no more than ten in total.

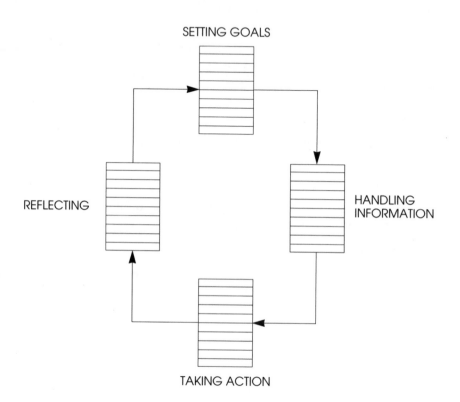

Ask a friend or a colleague who knows you well if they would agree with you.

Reflect on the mistakes you summarized earlier, and complete the following questionnaire.

SETTING GOALS

Do you normally have clearly defined goals at work?   YES   ?   NO

Are your personal goals clearly defined?   YES   ?   NO

Are your goals generally realistic?	YES	?	NO
Are all your goals achievable (not in conflict with each other)?	YES	?	NO
Are your goals timetabled?	YES	?	NO
Are your goals negotiated and agreed with others who are closely affected?	YES	?	NO

HANDLING INFORMATION

Do you tend to get bogged down in information and overwhelmed by detail?	YES	?	NO
Do you tend to act on the basis of the information available to you and stick to generally true rules-of-thumb?	YES	?	NO
Do you find that you latch onto important information easily available to you and, as a result, ignore other relevant information?	YES	?	NO
Do you focus on immediate needs or concerns and fail to look at longer-term consequences or side-effects?	YES	?	NO

TAKING ACTION

Do you find that you have acted hastily because of internal or external pressures (real or imagined)?	YES	?	NO
Do you generally refuse to act on intuition?	YES	?	NO
Do you tend to do too little or too late?	YES	?	NO
Do you often find you do completely the wrong thing?	YES	?	NO

MONITORING/REFLECTING

Do you tend to assume things are as they should be (i.e. actually happening or will happen) rather than checking?	YES	?	NO
Do you forget to reflect on a regular basis on what worked well and what went wrong?	YES	?	NO

What does this analysis tell you? If it helps, involve a friend or colleague in the discussion. Chapter 5 provides practical advice on how to learn from your mistakes.

CARL SNITCHER'S BIGGEST MISTAKE

Carl Snitcher, 50, is chief executive of the £24 million-turnover Paul Raymond Organisation, which has interests in clubs, theatres, publishing and property. He qualified as a lawyer at the University of Cape Town before moving to Britain in 1966. At first he worked for a firm of solicitors in the City, then became the legal officer at Equity, the actors' union, where he stayed for ten years, eventually becoming assistant general secretary responsible for mechanical media matters. He left the union in 1977 to become chief executive of the Paul Raymond Organisation.

My biggest mistake was name-dropping in order to impress my friends. It made me look an absolute fool.

In the early 1970s Edward Health's government was proposing to ban the closed shop and Equity was trying to negotiate an exemption. Our campaign was being masterminded by Gerald Croasdell, the union's general secretary at that time, who decided we should enlist the help of Lord Olivier.

He had recently been ennobled and hadn't yet made a speech in the House of Lords. We knew he was very well disposed towards Equity, so we approached him to see whether he'd be prepared to speak on our behalf. Gerald spoke to him on a Friday afternoon, then asked me to ring him as well to explain a bit about what was required. I'd never met the man, so I didn't know him at all. But I rang him at the National Theatre and he asked me to call him at his home in Brighton the following day when he'd had a chance to find out from other peers what he could and couldn't say.

That Saturday morning some friends of mine who I hadn't seen for a long time arrived from South Africa. I went to their hotel suite and while we were having tea I asked if I could use their telephone to make a terribly important call to Lord Olivier. The five of them sat quietly in the room listening to me and, of course, they could only hear my side of the conversation. It went something like this:

> 'Good morning Lord Olivier, it's Carl Snitcher. If you remember, I spoke to you yesterday afternoon about the industrial . . . no, Carl Snitcher. And you said . . . Carl, yes, Carl Snitcher. You were going to speak to Lord . . . no, with a "C". Carl. You were going to . . . Snitcher. S-N-I-T-C- . . .'

By this time people were just falling about on the floor. Here was I, trying to get through to this great man who obviously didn't know who the hell I was, and they thought I was an absolute twit. He didn't understand what I was talking about, and I came to the conclusion I must have woken him up.

My friends were just wetting themselves. I've never seen people laugh as much, and I was mortally embarrassed.

On the Monday, my colleagues and I had to go and see him at the theatre. I was actually scared at the prospect. We walked into his office and he was sitting with his feet up on the desk, wearing a brace. When Gerald introduced me, Olivier just said: 'You know, I did a film in Hollywood in the thirties. It was the worst experience of my life. The director's name was Snitcher . . . Schneider . . . Schitzer or something. He was a shit.' And that was it. No further conversation was directed at me, though I did try to butt in from time to time. Maybe he thought I was something to do with this horrible director.

In the end he made his speech and we got our exemption. But the point is, there was I, from South Africa, trying to impress my friends with all these terribly important people that I knew and the truth was it just didn't work.

The story of Carl Snitcher, mate of the great, has been told many times since. It was one of the most humiliating experiences of my life.

I learnt from that mistake that you have to be honest about who you do and do not know. You will be found out if you overstate your connections. I have never name-dropped since.

4

LESSONS LEARNED FROM MISTAKES

If you don't learn from your mistakes, there is no point in making them.

Anon

The value of a mistake lies not in the mistake itself, but in what you learn from it. Not all mistakes are bad for you. It is our, and others', assertion that there can be such a thing as the right kind of mistake, so long as the mistake was made in the right way, and lessons were learned from the experience. Having reviewed the mistakes people make in Chapter 3, in this chapter we will take a closer look at the lessons that were described by the 'My Biggest Mistake' authors.

LESSONS LEARNED

All the lessons reported were valuable to the authors and it is impossible to select the 'best' because each lesson made most sense to the person who actually made the mistake. Here are some examples to illustrate the kinds of lessons people said they learned, in their own words:

O   Getting carried away with the glamour of wanting to do something was nearly catastrophic.
O   I should have stuck to the knitting.
O   The amount of energy you have to devote to getting the right people is almost a full-time job in itself.
O   You can't ride two horses at once. Different businesses have different cultures.

O   If you are going into partnership, make sure you share the same goals and can work together to achieve them.

O   Pay attention to detail, especially when you are dealing with something outside your normal routine.

O   Never be complacent – you can make mistakes at any point in your business career.

OUR STUDY

We looked at the lessons closely, using an approach similar to the analysis of the mistakes. Here is the procedure we followed:

1   Two of the authors separately took 40 lessons and categorized them.
2   The categories were discussed and a common form of words was agreed to create a coding framework.
3   This coding frame was used to analyse the next 40 lessons by the two researchers working independently.
4   The coding was discussed, and the coding frame refined.
5   The coding frame was then used to code all lessons.

Again we found that some common themes emerged. These are described in Box 1 and the percentages are shown in Figure 4.1.

We would not say that all of the lessons that people learn will fit into these categories, but we do believe that the categories are a helpful framework. They give us a simple way of talking about the kinds of things that may be learned from making a mistake. As we've already said, we believe anything that makes it easier for us to talk about our mistakes has to be helpful.

So what, specifically, did people learn? We will examine some examples of the things people wrote in the 'My Biggest Mistake' series of articles in order to put some meat on the bones of these categories. The detailed findings are shown in Table 4.1.

DEFINE THE FOCUS OF THE BUSINESS

There were three different types of lesson which fell into the broad category of learning to define the focus of the business:

O   stick to the knitting
O   focus on customer needs
O   position the business.

BOX 1   WHAT LESSONS WERE LEARNED?

These categories of lessons were described in the 'My Biggest Mistake' series, on which we based our research described in Chapter 3.

Define the focus of the business

O   Stick to the knitting
O   Focus on customer needs
O   Position the business

Manage finances

O   Manage financial risks
O   Plan your finances

Prepare and plan

O   Think long term
O   Do your groundwork thoroughly

Get the way of working right

O   Correct structure
O   Effective processes

Deal with people effectively

O   Manage impressions
O   Work effectively with other people (internally)
O   Develop 'the right stuff'/working style
O   Work effectively with clients, customers and business partners

Miscellaneous/industry-specific

STICK TO THE KNITTING

The notion that organizations need to 'stick to the knitting' was one very clear theme among the lessons. This idea was popularized by the two management experts, who argue that companies need to identify and focus on their 'core competences'.[1] Here are a couple of examples from the 'My Biggest Mistake' series.

Michael Crosswell, now chairman of the Blue Arrow Group employment agency, described a lesson from early in his career. It was 1971 and Crosswell was a successful regional manager in the north-west with Coats Patons (now Coats Viyella). Just as he was considering moving on he was

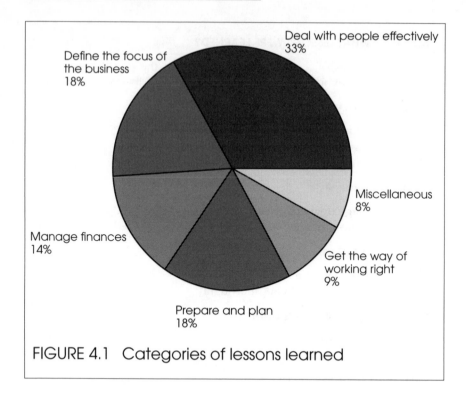

Deal with people effectively
33%

Define the focus of
the business
18%

Miscellaneous
8%

Manage finances
14%

Get the way of
working right
9%

Prepare and plan
18%

FIGURE 4.1   Categories of lessons learned

asked by his neighbour, who was recovering from a heart attack, to take over the running of a printing company. Crosswell describes himself as: 'young, feeling very brave, and thought I could do anything'. He quickly found, however, that he was out of his depth, permanently confused and panicked, and unable to learn fast enough to deal with the situation. The primary lesson for Crosswell was:

> When it comes to running a business, you've got to stick to what you know . . . And if you do find yourself exploring uncharted waters, make sure you do your research first.

A second example comes from Michael Peters, who headed the Michael Peters Group which was the first design company to be floated on the London Stock Exchange. For the first few years after flotation his company was one of the darlings of the stock market, but it all started to go wrong when the temptation to expand the business became too much. Peters describes two mistakes. First, looking for areas of related opportunity, rather than expanding the core business. Second, expanding too quickly.

TABLE 4.1   Percentage of lessons in each category

	%
Define the focus of the business	
Stick to the knitting	7
Focus on customer needs	6
Position the business	5
Manage finances	
Manage financial risks	10
Plan your finances	4
Prepare and plan	
Think long term	6
Do your groundwork thoroughly	12
Get the way of working right	
Correct structure	3
Effective processes	6
Deal with people effectively	
Manage impressions	6
Work effectively with other people (internally)	10
Develop 'the right stuff'/working style	10
Work effectively with clients, customers and business partners	7
Miscellaneous/industry-specific	8
Total=372	100%

The result was that the company moved from areas of the business that were very profitable to other areas that were much less well understood. The group very quickly got itself into difficulty. The company is now, according to Peters, back to basics:

> From now on, we'll be sticking firmly to what we know best, what gives us most pleasure and what gives our clients the best creative and financial results.

The moral of the story is that if you don't stick to the knitting, there is a risk of falling into the trap of being a jack of all trades, yet master of none.

FOCUS ON CUSTOMER NEEDS

One of the 'big ideas' for businesses in the 1980s and 1990s, particularly as western organizations tried to catch up with the Japanese, was that the customer is all-important. It is relatively unsurprising that focus on both internal and external customer needs was one of the categories of lessons learned.

John Garnett, who went on to be the director of the Industrial Society, describes his mistake which led to him being 'required to leave' his post after three years as personnel manager of ICI's plastics division, and return to a head office post. The chairman of the division told him that the division was in the business of making profits in plastics, while the board saw Garnett as being in the business of developing people. Garnett recognizes that he failed to make the point that in order to make profits in plastics, the division needed to call forth and use the gifts of its people. It lost him his job. For him, the lesson learned was:

> Try and sell ideas in relation to the objectives of those you're selling to, not your own objectives.

POSITION THE BUSINESS

The third type of lesson in this broad category relates to the importance to businesses of being 'in the right place at the right time'. In other words, the lesson is to position the business appropriately.

Caroline Charles set up the Caroline Charles Design Company in 1963 and quickly established herself as designer to the stars, with names such as Mick Jagger, Ringo Starr and Barbara Streisand on her client list. A big American company approached her and offered access to a large number of factories to enable her to start making clothes in quantity. Unfortunately things did not work out and she was told that the deal would only go ahead if the UK operation was shut down, with everything done from the States. Caroline Charles had to start again from nothing. She no longer even had use of her name; that had been sold to the Americans. In her own words the lesson was:

> For someone of 22 it is very nice to have America on your doorstep, but the biggest is not necessarily the best when it comes to nourishing a small company.

MANAGE FINANCES

The second broad category of lessons is about the importance of managing the financial side of the business effectively. Two particular themes emerged:

O   manage financial risks
O   plan your finances.

MANAGE FINANCIAL RISKS

Roger Young, the director-general of the British Institute of Management, describes a mistake from his early career as a merchant banker. Whilst working on the prospectus for a rights issue on behalf of a South African gold mining company, he realized that the company was in a position to become more profitable than was reflected in the share price. He bought tens of thousands of shares, although he did not have the money to pay for them. He was confident he would be able to sell the shares at a large profit before the time when he would have to pay for them. Sure enough, in one day, Young very quickly made a large paper profit. However, the next day saw 'a bolt from the blue that surprised the world': South Africa's cessation from the Commonwealth. Shares in the gold mining company fell below the price Young had paid for them. He was forced to sell everything he had to pay for the shares. Young learned what he calls one of life's most important lessons:

> Never bet more than you can afford to lose, even on a supposed racing certainty.

The lesson has led Young to avoid all risks where he could not evaluate the maximum downside, and influenced his decision not to become a Name at Lloyds of London.

PLAN YOUR FINANCES

Sam Wauchope, the managing director of Acorn Computers, describes a lesson he learned about the importance of cash flow. At a time when Acorn was pushing for growth, its largest distributor began to delay its payments. Wauchope was looking more to the promises of future growth rather than hard facts of the present and he allowed these debts to grow. Eventually the distributor went out of business, leading to a loss of around £1 million. The lesson was:

> Always keep an eye on the cash; no matter how well your business appears to be doing, if you're not turning it into cash, you've got a problem.

PREPARE AND PLAN

A third category of lessons learned were connected with preparation and planning, adding weight to the idea that excellence results from 90 per cent perspiration and 10 per cent inspiration. Here there were two themes:

O   think long term
O   do your groundwork thoroughly.

THINK LONG TERM

Robert Brooks, chairman of Brooks vintage car auction company, describes a mistake he made during his time with Christie's. He took time out from a sale that he was preparing in America in order to watch a grand prix. He was asked to set up a sale in New York, despite the fact that the market was going through a difficult time. Brooks assured the senior management at the New York office that he would do his best to try and make the most of a very difficult situation. He managed to put together a sale to be held in Madison Square Garden on a Tuesday. Shortly before the sale was due to take place it was decided to open for a brief viewing period on the Sunday afternoon. That weekend a friend of Brooks invited him to watch the Montreal Grand Prix. He took up the invitation, as 'everything seemed to be hunky dory in New York'. Unfortunately, whilst Brooks was leaning over a pit wall in Montreal watching grand prix cars hurtle past at 150 miles an hour, the chairman of the New York company, along with several other dignitaries, decided to view the sale. The chairman was not impressed and Brooks's absence turned out to be a great political faux pas. As Brooks himself described the lesson:

> You have to concentrate on more serious aspects of the business at times when it would be very easy to join in the fun.

A second example is from Paul Layzell, who describes a mistake he made as managing director of BMW (UK). Because of the huge success of BMW he failed to question the management process in the company. He described it as too hierarchical, too many layers of management, with managers only interested in their own area of responsibility. He recognized the need for a culture change that would encourage people to work together and to make decisions without always referring them upwards. The lesson Layzell learned is to think about the future, even in times of success. As he puts it:

> The time to look at a company's culture and effect necessary change is not when it's in trouble, but when it's doing well.

DO YOUR GROUNDWORK THOROUGHLY

Several people described how they had learned the hard way that failing to plan is planning to fail. David Arnold, the director of studies at Ashridge Management College, describes his biggest mistake when he was invited to be a guest speaker at the annual management conference of a clothing supplier. His brief was to get the company's managers thinking strategically about the clothing market. The clothing supplier relied on Marks & Spencer for more than 75 per cent of its sales. Arnold's talk was given a relatively low-key reception, so he decided to encourage more reaction by raising the level of challenge. He made rude comments about Marks & Spencer, saying the managers needed to adopt a different perspective. At the end of the session a senior director went up to Arnold and explained that the reason everyone had been so quiet was that one of M&S's head buyers had been sitting in the audience. He describes his mistake as assuming he understood why people were reacting the way they were. The lesson Arnold learned from this was:

> In meetings, conferences and presentations, always make sure you find out exactly who you are speaking to.

GET THE WAY OF WORKING RIGHT

There were two themes within this strand:

O   get the correct structure
O   get effective processes.

CORRECT STRUCTURE

Nick Temple, the chief executive of IBM (UK), describes a product development project in which he was involved. He was asked by the breweries to produce a special point-of-sale terminal for pubs. About 50 IBM people, plus subcontractors, were working on the product. During the course of developing the product there was a lack of focus. The terminal became so big and complicated that it was practically unworkable. It took two years to introduce a terminal into a pub and very few were ever sold. IBM learned the lesson from this and restructured operations so that there is always one person directly responsible for each product.

EFFECTIVE PROCESSES

Bruce Sinclair, the managing director of Dell UK, describes the mistake made in the launch of Dell Canada. The challenge was to run a national company in a country with two languages. Quebec, a predominantly French-speaking area, was an important market and the company was launched with a bilingual campaign. For instance, all sales and technical staff spoke English and French. However, the campaign was unsuccessful in Quebec. It was pointed out that the campaign was not really bilingual at all, because the telephones were answered in English. Dell had hired only English Canadians who could speak French, and no French Canadians. The lesson Sinclair learned was:

> You have to hire people from the marketplace you are servicing, even if you are based in a different country.

DEAL WITH PEOPLE EFFECTIVELY

The final broad category is perhaps the most difficult: deal with people effectively. Our research suggests four lessons that can help us to deal more effectively with others:

- O   manage impressions
- O   work effectively with other people (internally)
- O   develop 'the right stuff'/working style
- O   work effectively with clients, customers and business partners.

MANAGE IMPRESSIONS

It may sometimes seem harsh, but is nonetheless true, that impressions matter. The good news is that we can influence the impression others take away of us.

Linda King Taylor, managing director of LKT Manpower Services, describes her biggest mistake as trying to save money on a lecture trip to Singapore to promote her first book. Facing pressure from her bank manager to keep down costs in her newly established business, she chose to travel to Singapore on a cut-price fare. The plane made several stops, was twelve hours late, and her luggage was lost. Having travelled in grubby clothes, Taylor faced the prospect of delivering a lecture to 500 business-people wearing jeans and a T-shirt, and without any slides to support her message. As she put in her article, the way you travel, the way you arrive and the way you present yourself is entirely in your hands. Her lesson was:

> If you are expected to be first class on arrival, that's how you travel.

She now also carries a suit and any presentation tools as hand luggage.

WORK EFFECTIVELY WITH OTHERS

It seems obvious but sometimes the way we work with others is far from ideal and can lead to difficult situations.

Terry Gasking, a management consultant and associate of Ashridge

Management College, describes a mistake he made in giving his blunt view to a director of one of the world's largest computer companies. Gasking was asked by the sales and marketing director to endorse the positioning of a new microcomputer. As the head of a software development company supplied by the computer company he was close to the market, and actually thought the product was wrongly positioned. Gasking told the director this and gave a list of reasons why. He subsequently discovered that the director had placed the product in the market himself and had driven the entire campaign. Cooperation with the computer company very quickly ended and Gasking's company was forced out of business. As a management consultant he has faced similar situations and has learned to tell people what they need to know by putting his points 'as gently as possible'.

DEVELOP 'THE RIGHT STUFF'

By 'the right stuff' we mean those personal skills and qualities that make the difference. Here are a couple of examples.

Geoff Shingles, vice-president of Digital Equipment Corporation, describes a mistake he made in launching himself into the wrong career. In his early career as an engineer he realized that because he had no ambition to stand out probably meant he was in the wrong job. In Shingles' words, 'whatever career you choose, you need more than just enthusiasm to be successful'. Vital though it is, enthusiasm is no substitute for genius. He was lucky to realize fairly early on that he was not a genius in that field and that he needed to find another career in which he could use his talents to the full. Happily he was clearly successful in doing this in the commercial world.

Another example comes from David Wilkinson, the managing director of Alko Exports, who describes the importance of getting the motivation for doing something right. During his time as marketing manager for Del Monte he received a call from a headhunter. Interested in finding out how much he was worth somewhere else, he went for an interview, and was eventually offered a 45 per cent pay increase to move to another company. He accepted the offer, but quickly regretted his decision to put money first. The lesson for Wilkinson was that personal satisfaction is more important than anything else.

WORK EFFECTIVELY WITH CLIENTS, CUSTOMERS AND BUSINESS PARTNERS

Andrew Robertson, chief executive of WCRS advertising agency, describes the mistake he made in underestimating the intensive care a leading client needed. He was involved in persuading a client to stay with the agency. Six months later he was told the client had made the non-negotiable decision to appoint another advertising agency. The problem was that although the client had been persuaded not to go, in six months the agency had not done enough to persuade the client to stay. The lesson Robertson learned was:

> When the relationship with a client isn't strong, it's essential to check and double-check they are happy with the progress that is being made.

We have given examples of some of the lessons described in our study and elaborated on our categories of lesson. We will look at how many of these types of lesson were described in the *Independent on Sunday* articles.

RESULTS OF THE ANALYSIS

The five main categories described accounted for just over 90 per cent of all the lessons talked about in the articles. This 'hit rate' suggests that the framework is a fairly good way of talking about the lessons that people said they learned. The rest of the lessons were either specific to a particular industry or simply did not fit into these categories.

The details of these results may actually be less important than the broad headlines. The real value of the categories is that they provide a relatively robust way of talking about the lessons people said they learned in their 'My Biggest Mistake' articles. For example, it is clear that the largest number of lessons concerned dealing with other people. In our view the numbers don't actually matter. What is important is that these categories make it easier to talk about mistakes and the lessons learned.

In this chapter we have discussed some of the different types of lessons that can be learned from mistakes, for individuals and for organizations. We have discussed the mistakes described in our research.

The purpose of reflecting on these lessons learned from mistakes is to make it easier and more comfortable to talk about mistakes in a way that is positive, productive and likely to help us learn more effectively. This has been the underlying theme for Part One of this book, i.e. *facing up to mistakes*. Learning from mistakes is difficult precisely because it is so difficult to face up to them. We have shown that making mistakes is an essential part of learning. The frameworks we have developed from our research make it easier to talk about mistakes in a neutral way and to face up to them without guilt or anxiety. This is the first step in learning from mistakes.

Part Two describes practical things we can do to ensure that we learn from our mistakes, once we have faced up to them. As in Part One, we will focus on individuals and organizations. Our purpose is to identify how, in our personal lives and within our organizations, we can support the transition from a blame culture to a gain culture. The question we set out to answer is very simple: How can we harness the positive (as opposed to the destructive) power of mistakes?

REFERENCE

1 Prahalad, C.K. and Hamel, G. (1990), 'The core competence of the organisation', *Harvard Business Review*, May–June, pp.79–91.

DAVID ARNOLD'S BIGGEST MISTAKE

David Arnold is director of studies at Ashridge Management College and a marketing consultant for such multinationals as Merck, Alfa-Laval and Boots. After gaining degrees in English literature at University College London and in modern drama at London University, he began a career in publishing in 1979 as an editor for Mitchell Beazley. He moved to Ashridge in 1984 as marketing manager and later, after taking an MBA at City University, became a tutor on Ashridge's MBA course. His book, *The Handbook of Brand Management*, is published by Century Business.

My biggest mistake was failing to find out who was going to be in the audience before I gave a speech. It was two years ago, when I had been invited to be guest speaker at the annual management conference of a leading clothing supplier, a company that relied on Marks & Spencer for more than 75 per cent of its sales. My brief as guest speaker was to encourage the audience to think strategically about the changing market.

The conference was held at Gleneagles. I had to speak for an hour and a half to 70 managers and when I began they were very subdued. I decided to raise the level of challenge in order to encourage some reaction. When my first attempts proved unsuccessful, I turned to my last resort: I suggested that Marks & Spencer, their lifeline, was not the paragon of business success they thought it was.

Now this did spark some reaction, but the audience was still more subdued than most groups – so I actually started being rude about their beloved Marks & Spencer. I justified these insults by saying I needed to make them take a different perspective, and even commented that I suspected the reason they were being quiet was because they were very loyal to their leading customer.

I could see they were all thinking hard – they weren't asleep or anything – and I assumed they were thinking about company issues. But at the end of the session, when we took a break for coffee, a senior director sidled up and said he had something to tell me. He took me aside and informed me that the reason they had been so quiet was because sitting next to him in the front row was their chief customer in person: one of the head buyers of M&S. At that point, my heart hit my boots and I realized I had made the most awful error of judgement.

When I spotted the buyer I remember going to enormous efforts to avoid him. I managed to escape, but only at the expense of leaving my coat behind in the conference room where everyone had assembled after coffee. I couldn't face going back in. The other thing I couldn't face was sending the company an invoice for the agreed speaker's fee or for my expenses in travelling to Scotland.

Looking back, I remember there was a lot of fidgeting going on during my speech. I thought it was because I was talking about their most valued customer.

It was the squirming of the senior director in the front row that I remember most. Clearly he was trying to make a judgement about whether he should speak up and halt me in mid-flow. I think it would have been better if he had. The night before, I had joined them for dinner and had become quite chummy with a lot of them, which is probably why I thought I was safe in taking the risk of winding them up. But it was a mistake to assume I understood why people were reacting the way they were. It was a fatal assumption, because it was wrong. As a result, I was more critical about Marks & Spencer than I normally would have been, and certainly more than was necessary.

I still can't believe that, doing the job I do, I didn't find out who was there beforehand. I've had no communication with the company since, but the lesson to be learned is quite simple. In meetings, conferences or presentations of any sort, always make sure you find out exactly who you are speaking to.

PART TWO

HARNESSING THE POSITIVE POWER OF MISTAKES

❖

5

LEARNING FROM MISTAKES MADE BY ORGANIZATIONS

We are all involved in organizations of some kind at some point in our lives. For many of us, a large percentage of our time will be spent in one. For this reason it is important to examine how learning occurs in organizations and, specifically, what role our mistakes, individually and collectively, can play in the success or otherwise of our organizations.

THE LEARNING ORGANIZATION

Many authors, including journalists, academics and management consultants, have written widely on the subject of the learning organization in recent years. The phrase 'the learning organization' is beginning to take on a life of its own.[1,2,3,4] Training companies which used to offer organizational change through total quality management now offer change through 'becoming a learning organization'. Companies are even beginning to describe themselves as learning organizations in their recruitment advertisements. But what exactly is 'the' learning organization? Is it the same as 'a' learning organization, for some writers prefer this term? How do organizations learn and, indeed, is it possible to talk about organizations learning? Finally, how does the process of learning from our mistakes fit in with these ideas? There are six sections in this chapter:

O   What is 'the' learning organization?
O   What is 'a' learning organization?
O   How do organizations learn?
O   The role of mistakes

O   The Blame Culture
O   The Gain Culture.

WHAT IS 'THE' LEARNING ORGANIZATION?

Many people have tried to describe and define the nature of 'the' learning organization. Most modern management books which touch on organizational development or change include one or more definitions of it. As a result there are now dozens of formulations and definitions of what is required to reach the status of 'the' learning organization. In an earlier book, *Learning Organisations in Practice*, we examined over twenty different definitions of 'the' learning organization. We found four distinct themes which could be said to underlie the learning organization concept.[5]

The learning organization:

O   creates a vision for the future to guide and even inspire
O   acquires a capacity for continuous renewal and self-transformation
O   encourages and sustains the learning of *all* members
O   provides increasing satisfaction and fulfilment to *all* stakeholders.

These points are discussed in detail in *Learning Organisations in Practice*, and we will not elaborate further here, other than to re-emphasize the importance of the quality of working life and life in general in definitions of the learning organization. This is explored further in Box 1. We shall focus here on the ideas of Peter Senge,[6,7] the person most closely associated with 'the' learning organization.

Peter Senge's book, *The Fifth Discipline: The art and practice of the learning organisation*, has been instrumental in popularizing the notion. According to him:

> Learning in organisations means the continuous testing of experience and the transformation of that experience into knowledge – accessible to the whole organisation, and relevant to its core purpose.

Senge talks about learning in organizations as something to be encouraged as beneficial to the organization. Few would argue with this. Indeed the central theme of *this* book is that learning is invaluable, and mistakes are simply one (very effective) way to learn. But is *learning in organizations* the same as *the learning organization*?

The short answer is 'no'. Senge says that 'the' learning organization is an ideal to which organizations must aspire in order to survive and thrive in an uncertain and constantly changing world. As he puts it: 'The learning organisation exists primarily as a vision in our collective imagination.'

BOX 1   THE IDEAL ORGANIZATION

Imagine your ideal organization. What would it feel like to work in it? When we ask managers these questions, typically they give the following answers:

It would . . .

○   make me feel valued
○   make me feel like I am doing something worthwhile
○   be a caring cooperative environment where genuine openness and trust is prized
○   make me feel recognized and valued as an individual
○   be family-friendly and environmentally concerned
○   be effective; we would be successful in what we do
○   feel like we were pursuing excellence
○   feel like I was enjoying myself.

One of the goals of an organization intent on learning is to bring about conditions which produce feelings such as these. As Charles Handy[8] has said, this is not only because we believe people really would prefer to work in this kind of organization, but also because we believe that it is essential if managers are to tap into the talents and potential of all the people who make up the organization. One of the themes which distinguishes 'the' learning organization approach from other organizational change strategies is this emphasis on personal wellbeing as an economic necessity.

However, whilst the concept of the learning organization might be intangible, the benefits of aspiring to be the learning organization are said to be great. The likely consequences of aspiring to the learning organization are:

○   more satisfied customers
○   the gaining and sustaining of competitive advantage
○   an energized and committed workforce
○   effective management of change
○   a more truthful organization.

These benefits will come, he argues, because real change comes from collective thinking and understanding within organizations, communities and society, and this is what the learning organization represents. We can find nothing to disagree with in this argument. Organizations that do not learn to learn quickly enough and to make use of that learning will certainly stagnate, possibly as a prelude to complete organizational failure. However, this list of benefits and positive consequences for organizations which at first looks so impressive is perhaps too impressive, even too good to be true. Could it be that 'the' learning organization is being promoted as a 'cure-all' or panacea to the challenges faced by organizations at this time? After all, this is what has happened to previous management ideas such as organizational development, matrix management, total quality management, and business process re-engineering; all good ideas of their time which were originally clearly defined and carefully targeted at specific business problems, but which were blown up into snappy 'buzzwords of the year' by journalists and management consultants. The result is that they have become clichés.

OUR VIEW OF THE NATURE OF 'THE' LEARNING ORGANIZATION

We have for a long time expressed the view that there is, and can be, no such thing as 'the' learning organization. We have argued that there can be no one definition of the learning organization, for to specify exactly what it should be is to miss the point. To define an 'endpoint' or finishing line suggests that we can stop learning, and this goes against a learning orientation. Until recently we have preferred the terms 'learning organizations', or 'a' learning organization.

WHAT IS 'A' LEARNING ORGANIZATION?

The term 'a' learning organization seems less prescriptive. Allowing people in organizations to work out for themselves what being a learning organization means *to them* is perhaps a much more effective form of help than imposing on them a formal concept that someone else has created.

Of course, people have still tried to define 'a' learning organization. Here are two definitions which illustrate the range of thought in this area:

> A Learning Organisation is systematic, accelerated learning that is accomplished by the organisational system as a whole, rather than the learning of individual members within the system. Learning Organisations are able to transform data into value knowledge and thereby increase the long-term capacity.[9]

> A Learning Organisation is one which has a vision of tomorrow, seeing the people who make up the organisation not simply being trained and developed to meet the organisation's ends in a limiting and prescriptive

manner, but for a more expanded role. Once an organisation accepts that it wishes to enable or empower its personnel, the important issue which emerges is whether this empowering process is to be limited or to be permitted to drive the organisation. To curtail or limit the process cannot be said to be empowerment but simply permitted change and adaptation. Empowerment raises crucial issues concerning leadership, decision making and the ownership of activities and their results. It is these issues which lie at the heart of the Learning Organisation.[10]

In the first example, a learning organization is defined as one which ensures that 'things which are learned' are 'captured', understood, and distributed around the system so that the organization as a whole can benefit.

The second definition is much broader, encompassing leadership, decision making, ownership, empowerment and vision. In short, the issues any organization ought to be concerned with if it wishes to be successful. Already we find ourselves back with the problem of the term being used as a 'catch-all', well-meaning but ultimately meaningless idea.

After the publication of our book, we now realize that we made a mistake. Not only can there be no such thing as 'the' learning organization; the concept of 'a' learning organization may also be unhelpful. In our opinion, there can only be 'learning in organizations', or 'organizational learning'. We no longer believe that anyone can convert a whole organization to 'learning organization' principles. Whether the process of embedding the principles of learning into an organization may, ten or fifteen years later, have produced an organization which lives and breathes learning remains to be seen. However, for now, what we know can be done is to use the principles of learning, apply them in order to help people solve specific problems, and to help them learn how to solve or prevent these problems in the future. This is organizational learning in practice. (We describe some examples in Chapter 8.)

HOW DO ORGANIZATIONS LEARN?

Before we discuss the ways in which mistakes can contribute to organizational learning, we must explore the idea of learning in organizations further. How do organizations learn? Some authors have suggested that this is a nonsense question. For example, Professor Peter Herriot has said 'organisations don't learn . . . people learn'. The second half of this sentence is definitely true. The first half we would argue with. Whilst we must beware of talking about organizations as if they were alive, there is a sense in which organizations, as distinct from the people in them, can learn; for example, the manufacturing company which installs a computer network so that all mistakes made during the design process of its new products are recorded. As this database is built up, a store of useful information, a form of organizational memory, is developed, which individual people can access and utilize. However, here it is not any one person who has learned, but the cumulative effect of many people in the organization learning.

So if we accept the notion that organizations, as opposed to people, can learn, how does it happen? As you may expect, authors have suggested many approaches. This section summarizes some of the main ideas that have been put forward and shows how the transition from a blame culture to a gain culture is a fundamental requirement for organizational learning.

We start by assuming that people are willing and able to work. They do not always need to be told exactly what to do and how to do it. The job of a manager therefore is not one of control, but of creating the conditions and securing the resources people need to perform to the best of their ability. To support this a climate of curiosity, forgiveness, trust and togetherness is necessary. This is part of a gain culture; in our view, a prerequisite for learning in organizations.

ORGANIZATIONAL LEARNING AND CHANGE

We have discussed in some detail the emotional barriers we all put up which can prevent us from learning from our mistakes. These are the feelings of anxiety, and accompanying threats to our sense of self-esteem and identity, which may lead us to deny or hide our mistakes from others. Ed Schein[11] draws a parallel with organizational learning. He points out that for organizations to learn effectively they have to change, and all large-scale change in organizations produces a similar emotional response in those affected – anxiety, uncertainty and fear.

However, he suggests that the anxieties of change can be managed, and identifies three steps organizations must go through in order to learn successfully. (He has also outlined a set of actions to help organizations learn faster – see Box 2.) For successful learning, a key person or group within the organization must show people that the current way is wrong, help them consider the consequences of continuing in this way, and provide a 'safe' environment to try out the new way.

The first step is to provide evidence which shows people in the organization that what they are doing now is no longer right. It may well have worked in the past, but it will not work in the future. This could be at the level of the whole organization (e.g. 'We're making cars, but that is not where our real strength lies – we should be making electronic circuits for cars'); the function or department ('The way our department is organized

---

BOX 2   ED SCHEIN'S EIGHT STEPS TO HELP ORGANIZATIONS LEARN FASTER

Based on his experience working with organizations, and his theories on how they learn, Ed Schein has suggested eight practical steps to help organizations learn faster:

- ○ leaders must learn something new
- ○ a change management group must be created
- ○ the steering committee must go through its own learning process
- ○ the steering committee must design the organizational learning process
- ○ the steering committee must establish task forces to create specific change programmes
- ○ the task forces must learn how to learn
- ○ the steering committee must maintain communication throughout the process
- ○ mechanisms to support continual learning must be put in place.

Chapter 8 reviews some practical case studies where we have used a similar approach to help specific groups in organizations learn effectively.

---

is wrong – it's too hierarchical, and it's stopping creativity'); or the team or individual ('The way we are forecasting our customer demand is not working – we underforecast by 20 per cent for each of the last six months.')

The second step is to create an anxiety associated with continuing to do something which will eventually fail (e.g. 'If we carry on making cars like this, the company will be taken over within three years'; 'If we don't produce some creative ideas soon, our department will be outsourced.') Helping people to see the future this clearly overcomes their reluctance to learn and change (itself caused by anxiety) by making them understand the consequences of not changing. Of course, this is easier said than done. Evidence from studies of takeovers and acquisitions of organizations suggests that in the face of large-scale change many people, particularly those who have strong feelings of loyalty to their company, deny to themselves that the change is really happening. Only when it is too late (e.g. to learn a new skill or way of working to fit in with the new requirements) do they admit to themselves what has happened.

The third step is to create a psychologically safe environment. In plain

English, this means that staff must feel safe to practise, experiment, explore the new idea or way of working, and of course to make mistakes. In order for this to happen, senior managers must make it clear that such behaviour is acceptable and that mistakes will not only be tolerated, but that they are likely to hold valuable insights and should be shared. Line managers must act in a way that supports mistake making, rather than one which punishes mistakes. We are talking about the creation of a gain culture.

THE ROLE OF MISTAKES

Throughout this book we have tried to emphasize that mistakes, commonly thought of as 'bad things', can under certain conditions become 'good things'. The right kind of mistake can provide us with a powerful learning experience: 'When we screw up, we don't forget.' Also, if we want to develop our thinking, our expertise and skill, we need to experiment and take risks. When we truly experiment we will make mistakes; they are inevitable (and often lead to great insights). Finally, whatever our intention, whatever our goal, we are at some point in our lives going to make a mistake. The way we respond to the mistake, and the way those around us respond, will determine whether we (a) reflect on and learn from the mistake, and so ensure that we do not repeat it, or (b) hide, deny the mistake or blame someone else, and so ensure that no learning occurs and that the mistake will be repeated.

It follows, therefore, that learning in organizations can be enhanced if mistakes are managed in an appropriate way, or reduced if they are not. Poor handling of mistakes is associated with a 'blame culture' and the positive handling of mistakes with an organizational 'gain culture'.

THE BLAME CULTURE

Blame cultures are based on the *negative* power of mistakes (see Figure 5.1).

Making mistakes is unpleasant and threatens our self-esteem. We fear mistakes and their consequences, so we try to conceal our own and we discourage them in others.

If other people make mistakes we blame them, and to make ourselves feel better, we punish them for their mistakes. This, of course, is even more unpleasant for the victims than the experience of the mistake itself. It leads people to fear making mistakes even more, and the blame culture lives on and, indeed, thrives. Where there is a blame culture, we see

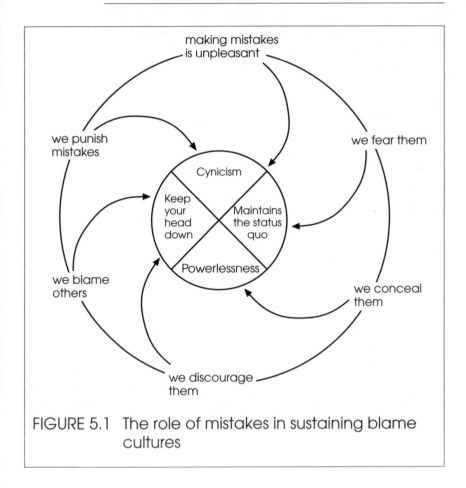

making mistakes
is unpleasant

we punish
mistakes

we fear them

Cynicism

Keep
your
head
down

Maintains
the status
quo

Powerlessness

we blame
others

we conceal
them

we discourage
them

FIGURE 5.1   The role of mistakes in sustaining blame
cultures

people with their heads down, afraid to challenge the status quo, cynical
yet powerless to break the cycle.

THE GAIN CULTURE

Chapter 2 identified the 'wrong' kind of mistakes – those that should
never happen even once, and which could 'sink the ship', and the 'right'
kind of mistake. We summarized the main features of the 'right' kinds of
mistakes as follows:[12]

○   the action leading to the mistake is well planned
○   the outcome of your action is uncertain

○   there is neither too much nor too little at stake
○   you can obtain rapid feedback
○   you can act on the result and make a change
○   the mistake is relevant to you and your goals.

If we, as managers within organizations, can create the right environment for the 'right type' of mistakes to occur, and we can react in an appropriate manner to other mistakes, then the benefits to the organization can be large. The gain culture is based on the positive power of the right kinds of mistakes (see Figure 5.2).

In a gain culture, people value the right kinds of mistake. They learn from them and avoid repeating them by sharing the lessons. The right

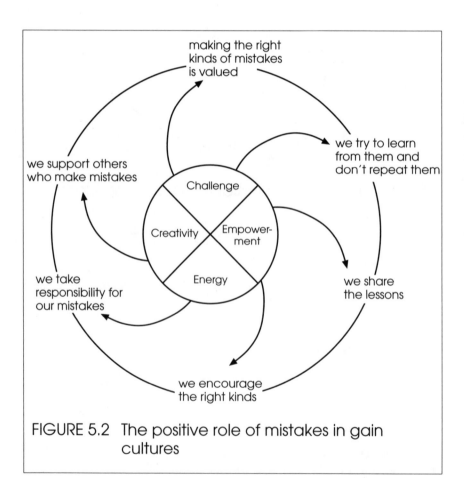

FIGURE 5.2 The positive role of mistakes in gain cultures

kinds of mistakes are encouraged, particularly by those in senior positions. When mistakes do happen, people take responsibility for their own mistakes and also support others who make them.

Where there is a gain culture, we see people being creative, challenging the status quo in a constructive way, and empowering others to learn effectively from mistakes.

Table 5.1 illustrates the different behaviours you might see in a blame culture and in a gain culture.

Individuals who manage mistakes appropriately will go a long way to creating the all-important gain culture which is required for organizational learning and development. Their actions are probably necessary but not sufficient for this to happen, however. Sitkin also argues that the right type of mistake must be *legitimized* in the organization, which can only happen when our organizational leaders stress the importance of the right type of mistakes and the way they are managed, and reinforce this message with their behaviour. As Soichoro Honda puts it:

> Many people dream of success. To me success can only be achieved through repeated failure and introspection. In fact success represents the one per cent of work which results from the 99 per cent that is called failure. (quoted in Sitkin, 1992)

Sitkin also quotes the President of Chapperel Steel:

> You've got to have an atmosphere where people can make mistakes. If we're not making mistakes, we're not going anywhere.

Executives and directors need to make it clear that 'the right kind of mistakes' are acceptable, if not desirable, and to 'walk the talk' for all employees to see. The organizational leader who can make the right kind of mistake, acknowledge it quickly and learn from it sends out powerful signals which become part of the folklore and established practice of the organization. Publicizing the right types of mistake helps provide concrete examples which describe what is acceptable to organizational leaders; what they mean by 'the right kind of mistake'. Similarly, the leader who can visibly manage a mistake made by a subordinate in an appropriate way sets a powerful example to all. They will have begun to create a gain culture.

In the present climate organizations are experiencing increased competition, putting them under pressure to secure consistently high short-term performance. This is often gained at the expense of longer-term objectives such as the need to acquire the capacity to adapt to rapidly changing environmental conditions. Success tends to breed short-term performance improvements, but mistakes provide the opportunity to adapt to change

TABLE 5.1   Blame and gain behaviours

Blame behaviours	Gain behaviours
• judging ('You were wrong')	• exploring ('What happened?')
• showing emotion ('I'm furious with you')	• remaining calm ('Try not to worry about it')
• reacting to what you think happened ('Surely you should have...')	• finding out exactly what happened ('Let's take this one step at a time...')
• blaming people for getting it wrong ('You should never have let this happen')	• focusing on the processes that allowed the mistake to happen ('What could have been done differently?')
• finding fault ('You only have yourself to blame')	• providing support ('This must be difficult for you but, don't forget, this has happened to us all')
• focusing on effects ('This is going to cause enormous problems for me')	• focusing on causes ('What I want to focus on is all the things that enabled this to happen')
• assuming the person should feel guilty/be contrite ('You really only have yourself to blame')	• assuming the person wants to learn ('What are the main lessons for us?')
• seeing mistakes as something that must be avoided ('This must never happen again')	• seeing mistakes as part of a learning process ('We can learn a lot from this')
Other blame behaviours?	*Other gain behaviours?*

and to build organizations' capacity to deal with unknown future changes. Mistakes provide opportunities for long-term performance improvement, in contrast to the short-term focus of learning from success. In short, learning to learn from mistakes is a vital part of organizational learning.

REFERENCES

1 Pedler, M., Burgoyne, J. and Boydell, T. (1992), *The Learning Company*, Maidenhead: McGraw-Hill.
2 Garratt, B. (1990), *Creating a Learning Organisation*, London: Institute of Directors.
3 Dixon, N. (1994), *The Organisational Learning Cycle: how we can learn collectively*, Maidenhead: McGraw-Hill.
4 Thurbin, P.J. (1994), *Implementing the Learning Organisation: the 17-day programme*, London: FT/Pitman.
5 Pearn, M.A., Roderick, C. and Mulrooney, C. (1995), *Learning Organisations in Practice*, Maidenhead: McGraw-Hill.
6 Senge, P. (1990), *The Fifth Discipline: the art and practice of the learning organisation*, New York: Doubleday.
7 Senge, P., Roberts, C., Ross, R., Smith, B. and Kleiner, A. (1994), *The Fifth Discipline Fieldbook*, London: Nicholas Brearley.
8 Handy, C. (1993), *Managing the Dream: the learning organisation*, London: Gemini Consulting.
9 Marquardt, M. and Reynolds, A. (1994), *The Global Learning Organisation: gaining competitive advantage through continuous learning*, New York: Irwin.
10 Stahl, T., Nyhan, B. and D'Aloja, P. (1992), *The Learning Organisation: a vision for human resource development*, EUROTECNET Technical Assistance Office.
11 Schein, E. (1993), 'How can an organisation learn faster? The challenge of entering the green room', *Sloan Management Review*, Winter.
12 Sitkin, S.B. (1992), 'Learning through failure: the strategy of small losses', *Research in Organisational Behaviour*, 14, pp.231–266.

DAVID BRUCE'S
BIGGEST MISTAKE

David Bruce, 42, failed his maths 'O' level five times before leaving school to work for a brewery. In 1979 he came off the dole queue to open the Goose and Firkin pub in London after raising a loan against his home. By 1988 he had built a chain of 18 pubs which he sold for £6.6 million, intending to retire with his £2 million share. But he could not resist going back into business. He is now trading as Inn Securities and building up a chain of Hedgehog and Hogsheads pubs outside London.

My biggest mistake was not paying proper attention to my accounts in the early days of the Firkin pubs. We had opened the Goose and Firkin in London in 1979 and I was working 18 lousy hours a day, seven days a week, brewing the beer in the cellar and surviving on adrenalin. I had eight staff and a part-time book keeper.

Everybody said the pub would not work, but people were queueing to get in. It was tremendously exciting and I was on a complete high. The tills were ringing, my break-even point was £2,500 a week but the pub never made less than £4,500.

So why, I thought, if one has created this extraordinary thing, should one scuttle back home to Battersea and spend hours doing boring old paperwork? The turnover was so good I did not even bother with profit-and-loss accounts. (And you have to bear in mind that I did not have a natural aptitude for figures.)

In May 1980 I opened the Fox and Firkin in Lewisham. I trained a brewer to look after the Goose, but he promptly broke his leg, leaving me to deal with both pubs. There was even less time to do paperwork. Then I opened another pub in London, and because the experts doomed us to failure I thought it would be easier if the pubs traded under separate companies. Each one had a different accounting year – it was a good lesson in how not to run a business.

By the time we had opened our fourth pub in 1981, our solicitors, Bishop and Sewell, had watched our progress with great interest and assumed we were incurring a hideous tax bill, so they suggested we met with accountants Touche Ross. My wife Louise and I went along with what little financial information we had, plus a couple of audits which showed we had traded at a loss from day one.

In fact, while the turnover for the first year was £1 million, we had made losses of £86,000. One of its corporate finance partners said that if I did not appoint a chartered accountant to the board as financial director immediately we would go bust within a couple of months. So I took on someone from a leading brewery who introduced systems such as stock control and weekly profit-and-loss accounts.

But that did not solve the immediate problems. Touche Ross also said I would have to sell one of the pubs, the Fleece and Firkin in Bristol, because it was costing too much time and money. Reluctantly I put it on the market.

By now it was obvious that I should have appointed a finance director at the beginning. The bank was getting nervous, my borrowings were rising and I was not producing a profit. If the bank had pulled the rug we would have gone down personally for £500,000. Touche Ross advised me to sell a small percentage of the equity, which of course I did not want to do.

Eventually I struck a satisfactory deal with 3i (Investors in Industry) which bought 10 per cent of the business and gave us a loan. Better cash control enabled us to turn a loss into profit, and the following year, on a turnover of £1.6 million we showed a profit of £47,000.

Touche Ross, who charged us under £5,000 to sort out the problem, has done my audits ever since. Paul Adams, our managing director, is the resident chartered accountant. He has kept costs down and introduced budgets which the staff can stick to.

In hindsight the solutions were obvious, but I was a victim of my own success. If the turnover had not been so good I would have realized a lot sooner how close I was to bankruptcy.

6

CULTIVATING INTELLIGENT MISTAKES IN A GAIN CULTURE

In today's organizations often the only source of competitive advantage is innovation. Successful companies need to change more quickly than the world around them and, specifically, more quickly than their customers and competitors. The only way for organizations to change in this way, to learn to do new things, is to constantly renew themselves and innovate. The only way that innovation will happen is if committed and energized people push against the inertia inherent within all organizations and actually try out their ideas. They have to 'do' something, to make things happen and to experiment.

Tom Peters has said that the chances of any innovation working well first time in an organization are minimal.[1] The only course of action left therefore is to make mistakes, and to make mistakes faster and faster. Peters has called on organizations to speed up the mistake-making process so that original innovations can be tested, mistakes can be made, valuable information can be learned, and ideas can be progressed quickly into workable solutions, products and services. The challenge for all organizational leaders therefore is how to create the conditions in which fast mistake making is not only tolerated, but is positively encouraged. How do managers move from the common experience of a blame culture, where mistakes are punished and discouraged, and innovation stifled, to create a gain culture where the opposite is true?

CREATING A GAIN CULTURE

In *Learning Organisations in Practice*[2] we identified six aspects of an organization which combine to produce an environment or culture which is supportive of learning. We created a framework, known by its acronym INVEST (see Figure 6.1), which emphasizes the proactive, sometimes painful, need to yield longer-term benefits. This framework provides practical ways to move towards a gain culture.

INSPIRED LEARNERS

Every organization needs people who are inspired learners – who put in extra effort and 'go the extra mile' to do things right; who experiment, trial, test, make mistakes and improve on how things are done. It is particularly important that the organization's leaders set a prime example. They must be able to make and show that they can learn from the 'right' type of

I	Inspired learners
N	Nurturing environment
V	Vision for a desired future
E	Enhancement of learning
S	Supportive management
T	Transforming structures

FIGURE 6.1 Six features of a gain culture

mistakes, and they must regard questioning, testing and challenging as the norm. They must be confident enough to admit and review their own mistakes, and to be skilful at learning from them.

NURTURING ENVIRONMENT

A nurturing environment is necessary to facilitate learning where there is open and honest feedback, where creative (generative) thinking is encouraged, mistakes are recognized and learned from, and where people are developed to their full potential. This aspect of the framework comes closest to capturing the notion of a gain culture. However, we find the INVEST framework as a whole is more valuable than any single aspect in helping us move from blame to gain.

VISION FOR A DESIRED FUTURE

For mistakes to be utilized in the most efficient manner, a vision for the future is required – one that encompasses an organizationwide approach to challenge, experiment and learn from mistakes. This vision may be communicated in terms of widely understood and accepted missions and values that place a strong emphasis on a high regard for individual and organizational learning.

ENHANCEMENT OF LEARNING

The systematic and intentional use of the right kinds of mistakes, and the utilization of enhanced learning techniques and methods, are essential. Possible methods include: systems thinking, scenario planning, paradigm busting, learning laboratories, skunkworks, computer modelling, and other simulations where making mistakes is crucial to effective learning.

SUPPORTIVE MANAGEMENT

The whole culture of fast, continuous mistake making, learning and improvement can only be maintained if there are supportive managers who understand that a key part of their role is to encourage learning in others; who understand the nature of learning and the critical importance of having room to make mistakes, and who have the skills to facilitate learning from mistakes using gain behaviours and avoiding blame behaviours.

TRANSFORMING STRUCTURES

Finally, transforming structures are necessary to prevent the organization becoming bureaucratically stagnated and functionally and divisionally fragmented. They will also enable the organization to adapt flexibly in the face of external change, and to adapt not just to present circumstances, but to be ready to adapt continually in response to changes in its external environment. Multifunctional customer-focused groups, strategic business units, flat organizations, inverted pyramids and intranets, all help break down the traditional pattern of hierarchical, centralized, functional 'silos' that are too slow and inflexible to meet the demands of today's world.

We will now describe each aspect of the INVEST framework in more detail and discuss how the positive power of mistakes can be harnessed in order to maximize innovation and learning in organizations.

INSPIRED LEARNERS

The first important ingredient is the extent to which everyone is motivated and confident enough to try new methods, to make mistakes and to learn continuously. One of the initiatives the Rover Group has used to produce inspired learners was the creation in 1990 of a separate business unit called the Rover Learning Business. During its existence, it served two specific purposes. It communicated to the workforce that Rover was serious about helping people to become inspired learners, and it provided a mechanism to achieve this. On top of some vital policy changes such as the move to single-status employees, several specific initiatives were implemented:

- O   job development programmes
- O   skill development courses
- O   a personal development grant
- O   distance learning and Open University
- O   team work and discussion groups
- O   computer-based learning
- O   coaching, counselling and mentoring
- O   liaison with local organizations.

In 1996, over £35 million was spent on learning throughout Rover. The INVEST acronym seems increasingly apt!

Allowing and encouraging people to seize opportunities for learning from experience and from mistakes, and to be fully committed to self-development, are clearly vital ingredients (see Box 1). We tend to learn most when we are excited by what we are doing, taking pride in our work, feeling involved and fully participating in decisions that affect us. It also helps if we are valued, and if the value we are adding through our mistakes and learning is acknowledged. In these circumstances most of us

---

BOX 1   SIX WAYS TO ENCOURAGE INSPIRED LEARNERS

○   Make an open commitment to help everyone learn both at work and in their private lives.

○   Make efforts to build people's confidence to learn.

○   Set aside time and processes for capitalizing on the benefits of learning from mistakes and experience.

○   Give everyone the right to question and challenge the status quo and to expect full answers.

○   Give help to those who need it in learning to learn.

○   Give everyone a personal development plan which contains specific reference to formal learning objectives and routinely review the plans.

---

want to take charge of our own learning, if we are given the opportunity to do so. Rover maintains that everyone has two jobs: first, to carry out the tasks their jobs require and, second, to learn to do them better on a continuing basis.

It is not only commercial organizations that need inspired learners, it is the whole of society. The Royal Society of Arts' enquiry into continuous learning concluded that for our countries and communities, a commitment to continuous learning pays.[3] In a second report entitled *Profitable learning* a ten-point action plan was presented to help create a learning society in the UK,[4] one in which the vicious circle of the twentieth century – low productivity and profits, low investment, low standards, low skills – will be replaced by the virtuous circle of the twenty-first century – high aspirations, high standards, high skills, high satisfaction, high productivity (see Figures 6.2 and 6.3).

The report notes that at its best, learning is continuous and often informal; existing models of education and training overemphasize the initial and formal aspects of learning. The report's three main findings are:

○   that learning pays

○   that in a learning society the principle of lifelong learning should be the informing idea of education

○   that it is the supply side of education and training that must change first if a true learning society is to be created.

Later work by the RSA led to the launch of the Campaign of Learning – an attempt to support us in becoming a society of inspired learners.

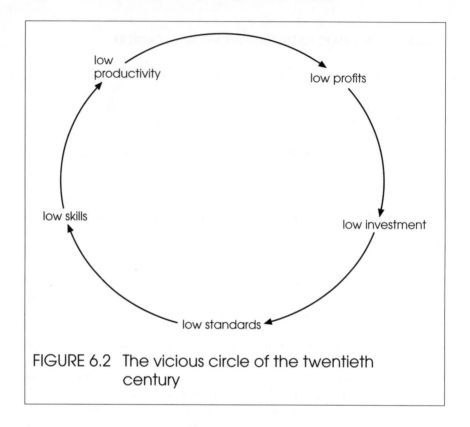

FIGURE 6.2   The vicious circle of the twentieth
century

NURTURING ENVIRONMENT

The environment of an organization is expressed most powerfully not through articulated values, mission statements and the like, but through displayed behaviour which is consistent with them. The values of an organization should support mistake making and continuous learning; they should encourage challenges to the status quo, questioning of assumptions and probing established ways of doing things. Testing, experimenting, learning from mistakes, exploration and reasoned debate should be valued activities. In addition the organizational environment should recognize the wholeness and the dignity of people who have fears, doubts and uncertainties, and who would prefer to be treated with openness and honesty (see the case studies in Chapter 8). Part of this for us is to recognize that no one has all the answers and that everyone makes mistakes. In fact mistakes, especially if they are 'the right kind', are a good sign of a healthy organization.

If the prevailing culture is secretive and works through command and

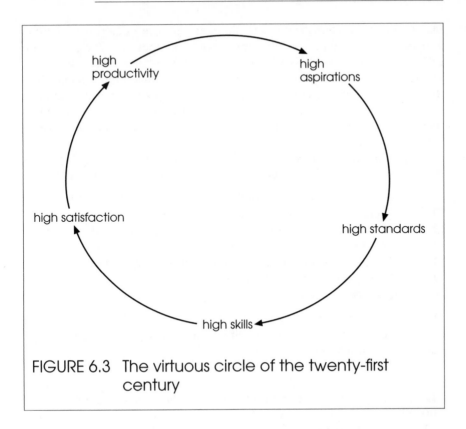

FIGURE 6.3 The virtuous circle of the twenty-first century

control where people are expected to do passively what they are asked to do and nothing else, there will be a prevailing atmosphere of cynicism and apathy. In this situation most of us will do as little as we can get away with, and will not take steps to improve things.

It is very difficult for our managers to say 'question me, challenge me, disagree with me, do it better than me'. If they have been raised and promoted on the basis of their successes, it is unlikely that they are going to admit that someone else has thought of a 'better' way than them. Being challenged, even by a very junior member of staff who could not possibly be construed as a 'threat' in any practical sense to a manager's position, can be perceived as a threat to his or her self-esteem. Managers have been known to react very violently in such situations; an understandable response but not a constructive one, and not one which encourages people to make the right kinds of mistakes. In fact, such a reaction could be taken as a symptom of a blame culture.

According to Harvard professor Chris Argyris, it is difficult to get senior managers to learn.[5] Smart people, as he puts it, have an infinite capacity to blame others, to rationalize away failure, and they are defensive. There is a marked difference between the way people say they are acting (what he calls 'espoused theory'), and the way they really act (what he terms 'theory-in-use'). Managers at the top need to evaluate and change their theories-in-use, to overcome their tendency to reason defensively and to recognize the negative consequences of that defensive reasoning. Only then will they begin to be able to learn. Only then will they be able to learn from their mistakes.

Argyris developed this theme of defensive behaviour. He identified practical ways in which managers can overcome defensive reasoning:

O   make a diagnosis of the problem
O   connect the diagnosis to actual behaviour
O   show them how their behaviour creates organizational defences
O   help them to change their behaviour
O   change the defensive routine that reinforced the old behaviour
O   develop new organizational norms and culture to reinforce the new behaviour.

The answer is not to make laws against organizational defensive routines; rather, individuals must become self-managing and create organizations that reward self-responsible actions.

People need to check that in both stated values and in actual behaviour individual, group and total organizational learning is valued as a prime asset and that there is a general climate of mutual respect, openness and trust. The typical signs that would say to people 'yes, mistakes are treated as learning opportunities here' are things like: reflection and review are built into work routines; people can experiment without suffering unpleasant consequences; provision is made for incidental learning and learning from everyday experience; and everyone is encouraged to learn from one another, by making their thinking explicit, and by sharing it with colleagues.

VISION FOR A DESIRED FUTURE

It is widely recognized that a clear, preferably shared vision of what an organization is trying to achieve is critical to organizational success. This statement is equally true for the creation of a gain culture. Part of the vision should include the organization's capacity to identify, respond to, and benefit from future possibilities. The vision should recognize the importance of learning at individual, group and system level, including learning from mistakes. This will enable the organization to transform itself continuously and acquire resilience in an increasingly unpredictable world.

Peter Senge[6] has argued that the authority of top management should be based not on the exercise of power but on the respect and inspiration that comes from serving the organization as a community with a vision. The meaning that comes from a vision should not be handed over, but created from within.

Leaders, he says, are designers, teachers and stewards. They need new skills, the ability to build shared vision, to bring to the surface and challenge prevailing mental models. In short, leaders who believe in and try to encourage organizational learning are responsible for building organizations where people are continually expanding their capabilities to shape their future.

This kind of fundamental shift involves changes to the essence of organizations.[7] The key issues are identified for top managers who set out to implement fundamental changes. They are a clear vision of the desired end state; a conscious decision to move to a learning mode, where both learning and doing are equally valued; and a clear commitment from the top to making a personal investment in achieving the vision. Organizational leaders have a crucial role to play: their behaviours must be congruent with the articulated vision; they must make a personal commitment to that vision, and they must enrol the commitment of other key players. To change the essence, top managers must: create and set the vision; communicate the vision; build commitment to the vision; and organize people and what they do so that they are aligned with the vision. This alignment requires the integration of roles, systems and rewards. The fundamental role of the leaders of thriving organizations is to create the conditions that produce commitment and creative actions by the people in the organization.

An organization needs to consider whether the vision is clear and whether it is understood and accepted by everyone. Does the vision emphasize the importance of learning to cope with whatever the future brings? Does it emphasize the ability to self-transform continuously? Does the vision make any reference to actually shaping rather than merely responding to the future? Has an action plan or road map to achieve the organization's vision of its future been put in place? Is everything that is done consistent with the vision and is everyone mindful of it on a daily basis?

TABLE 6.1   Techniques to enhance learning

Organizational	Individual
Learning laboratories	Systems thinking
Scenario planning	Open or distance learning
Historical review	Action learning
Learning networks	Testing assumptions
Process mapping	Learning contracts
Strategic alliances	Dialogue techniques
Benchmarking	Learning to learn workshops
Skunkworks	Support mechanism
Microworlds	Creative learning
Search conferences	Experimentation
Open systems technology	Building conceptual models
	Questioning
	Active reflection

ENHANCEMENT OF LEARNING

There are many methods and techniques to enhance learning in organizations. Some methods are wholly organizational in scope, others encourage and sustain organizational learning through enhancing the learning of individuals (see Table 6.1).

Here we will look more closely at three of the organizational techniques. The next chapter examines a selection of the more individual techniques.

LEARNING LABORATORIES

Learning labs and microworlds in particular make use of computers and multimedia technology as learning tools which are being used less for the sole provision of access to information and increasingly for the enhancement of learning.

The technology is already available. The challenge is essentially conceptual rather than technical. Learning laboratories are an innovation in infrastructure, a practice field where teams surface, test, and improve their mental models, where computer simulation tools like management flight simulators can be used. A microworld is any simulation in which people can live in the simulation, running experiments, testing different strategies, and building a better understanding of the real world which the microworld depicts. A management flight simulator involves developing a theory about the organization itself, reframing the shared mental model of the organization, by redesigning the computer model that represents the organization.

We are just learning how to successfully design and implement learning laboratories. It is a task which must involve the organization's leaders because it involves redefinition of managerial work which includes accountability for producing results and for producing knowledge about how the results were produced.

LEARNING THROUGH SIMULATION

Computer simulations and games have been used in organizations so that people learn from mistakes without having to experience the painful costs of real-world mistakes. They have been used to help managers learn about how organizations work, but in a safe world which allows people to make mistakes without doing any real harm. This work is largely associated with the Massachusetts Institute of Technology (MIT), and people such as Jay Forrester and Peter Senge, along with associates such as Arie de Geus.

The reasoning behind the approach is as follows. Organizations and the conditions (market, economic, political) in which they operate are closely related. Whenever there is a change in the economic climate, the organization will be affected. Whenever a large organization takes decisive actions, the environment will be changed. So top managers have to make difficult decisions without really knowing what will happen as a result. They very likely have only one shot at getting it right; if they make a mistake, they will not be allowed the luxury of learning from it. Wouldn't it be useful to let them try out their ideas in safety and make their mistakes before they needed to take the decision in real life?

Royal Dutch Shell faced this very problem at the end of the 1960s. What might the future hold? What might it look like? What were the most likely future scenarios, and how might they affect Shell if they happened? And what decisions should Shell's leaders take? With an organization as large as Shell, it inevitably takes time to adapt to new conditions; time that it could not afford.

Arie de Geus worked in the strategic planning unit at Shell. He wanted to find a way to understand the future and its effect on Shell. He wanted to find a way for the organization to learn about itself and its future. De Geus was influenced by Piaget and his study of children learning. The best answer seemed to be to allow managers to 'play' and experiment, just as Piaget's children had. However, this was impossible within an organization. De Geus needed a safe environment for his managers to learn comfortably in. He found it through a collaboration with MIT.

MIT, and particularly Jay Forrester, had been working for some time on detailed computer simulations of business environments. These described the organization and the market as complex and interrelated, and attempted to model the relationships between the two. De Geus and his fellow planners produced various scenarios (e.g. oil crisis vs no oil crisis). They then modelled them on a computer, which enabled them to 'play' with various actions to see what effect those actions would have. They made many 'mistakes', providing important information about what not to do under various conditions. The planners learned from their mistakes and increased their understanding of the way the oil economy worked. As a result, Shell had a strategy in place for when the oil crisis hit in the early 1970s. It was able to act quickly, and saved itself a lot of expensive problems.[8]

Just like people, organizations make mistakes. The only difference is more people are involved, so the mistakes can be even bigger; and they also become harder to talk about. Our experience tells us that learning from mistakes at the organizational level is even harder than it is for us as individuals. We will now look at how organizations can ensure they make the right kinds of mistakes from which they can continue to learn. We believe this is the only way in which organizations can avoid the lethal cocktail of the three Cs of complacency, conservatism and conceit. Organizations simply *must* make the right kinds of mistakes, and learn from them; or else they will surely die.

HISTORICAL REVIEW

The historical method examines mistakes that organizations have made in order to understand them, and learn from them. For example, Hal Hartley looked at mistakes at IBM, Harley-Davidson and Days Inns.[9]

Record losses at IBM

In 1993 IBM reported the largest annual loss in American history with a 1992 deficit of $4.97 billion. The cost in people was also staggering. Since 1985, IBM had laid off 100,000 people, and had restructured five times. For so long IBM had been the blue-chip company that could do no wrong as far as investors were concerned. At its peak, it was the largest computer manufacturer in the world, employing 350,000 people worldwide. In 1991 sales revenues had reached $67 billion. In 1989 it ranked first among all US firms in market valuation, fourth in total sales and fourth in net profits. Everyone admired and revered IBM, but in 1992 everything changed.

According to Hartley, IBM's problems were threefold: it had become a cumbersome organization, becoming more and more bureaucratic as it grew, with a corresponding resistance to change; it had an over-central-ized management structure, slow reaction times and no incentive to people lower in the organization to do things differently; finally, it had fallen foul of the three Cs mindset of vulnerability – complacency, conservatism and conceit.

As a result IBM had become overdependent on high-margin main-frames, had neglected software and service, had become accustomed to bloated costs, and was experiencing diminishing payoffs from its massive R&D expenditure.

Dramatic loss of market share at Harley-Davidson

Harley-Davidson, the American motorcycle manufacturer, was founded in 1903, and dominated its market. By the early 1960s Harley had destroyed almost all its competition and had 70 per cent of the US motorcycle market.

In the space of five years, this had slipped to 5 per cent. At that time the total market was expanding quicker than it had ever done before. The market grew from 400,000 bikes in 1960 to four million in 1971. Unfortunately for Harley-Davidson, this was thanks to Honda instituting a new strategy to expand the demand for motorcycles. It did this by emphasizing lightweight cycles and aiming marketing efforts at new customers. Harley's sales remained steady during this time, which meant it was not getting any of the new customers created by Honda. From 70 per cent down to 5: few companies have experienced such a shattering of market share as this.

Growth for growth's sake at Days Inns

Days Inns made the mistake of letting its standards slip for the sake of growth. Founded in 1970, there was a leveraged buyout of the company in 1984. The new owners wanted the most rapid growth. Costs were cut wherever possible, even when this meant dropping standards. The pursuit of growth led to the acquisition of Ramada and Howard Johnson. By 1992 Days Inns was the world's largest hotel franchiser with 134,000 rooms. The company quickly ran into difficulties because, having oversupplied the market for hotel rooms, its failure to maintain standards put it at severe risk.

Other examples which may be familiar are Hoover's disastrous sales pro-motion and the new Coca-Cola formula which went badly wrong. There are some common factors which have led to organizations running into trouble, for example size, bureaucracy and poor planning. And of course the good news is that there are also some important lessons to come out of these mistakes. One of the biggest lessons concerns the way organiza-tions grow and expand.

Hartley's research suggests six clear lessons for organizations about growth (summarized in Box 2).

BOX 2   LESSONS ABOUT ORGANIZATIONAL GROWTH

O   Growth targets must be within capabilities.

O   Keep it simple and consistent.

O   Focus resources to make the most of expansion opportunities.

O   Don't neglect other parts of the organization during expansion.

O   Beware of rapidly expanding markets.

O   Decentralized management facilitates rapid growth.

SUPPORTIVE MANAGEMENT

In an organization that is dedicated to optimizing learning, a prime role for managers is to encourage and sustain learning in others with the aim of achieving improved performance at individual, group and organizational level. Managers should see their main role as facilitating and coaching rather than commanding and controlling.

We've already discussed the notion of defensive reasoning. People reason defensively to avoid vulnerability, risk, embarrassment and the appearance of incompetence. Managers must demonstrate a new level of self-awareness, candour and responsibility if they are to develop employees who think constantly and creatively about the needs of the organization with as much intrinsic motivation and as deep a sense of organizational stewardship as any company executive.

Ask the following questions to identify whether or not you have supportive managers:

O   Are managers truly receptive to new ideas, regardless of where they come from?

O   Do they routinely behave in accord with espoused values?

O   Do managers understand that their prime role is to coach and develop, rather than control and monitor, and are they competent to carry out this role?

O   Is time really allocated for reflection and review, especially when the organization is under pressure?

O   Do managers understand the learning process and in particular the importance of mistake making?

O   Are they actively involved in supporting employees to learn and develop continuously?

O   Are they similarly actively learning and developing themselves?

O   Do they encourage dialogue and work with mindsets and paradigms?

O   Is empowerment genuinely believed in and practised?

O   Do managers genuinely believe organizational performance will be improved if decisions are pushed as far down the organizational hierarchy as possible?

TRANSFORMING STRUCTURES

Much has been written on the subject of how organizations have become unwieldy, bureaucratic and slow to respond. They can become too detached from the external world and their customers, especially in terms of where decisions and policy are made.

Ricardo Semler[10] provides a good example of the enabling role of transforming structures. He transformed his father's business, 'Semco' in Brazil, from a traditional pyramidal structure of twelve management layers to that of a structure based on three concentric circles. Among the changes introduced in the past eleven years is the abolition of rule books, policies and receptionists/PAs/secretaries and the treatment of all employees as responsible, trustworthy adults. Workers set their own production quotas; managers set their own salaries; everyone has a vote on big decisions and profit sharing and managers are evaluated six-monthly by those who work below them. As Semler puts it: 'Bosses don't have to be parents and workers don't act like children.' The company is organized in a way that encourages and rewards innovation, learning and development.

When thinking about transformative structure, consider the following questions:

O   Are there only as many managerial and supervisory layers as are necessary?

O   Are managers in the conventional sense needed at all?

O   Is work organized into self-managed or self-directed teams wherever possible with a high degree of autonomy and self-control?

O   Is work defined in terms of objectives and assignments with the minimum of rules?

O   Does the organization ensure that knowledge and ideas move quickly to where they are needed, even across functional boundaries and business units?

O   Is centralized control kept to a minimum?

O   Is everyone given as much autonomy as possible? Are customer-focused multifunctional teams the norm?

O   Is the top management team itself functionally diverse?

In this chapter we have tried to clarify what we mean by a gain culture. We identified practical ways of moving towards a gain culture using our INVEST framework for a learning organization. We discussed how each of these six areas of the framework can harness the positive power of mistakes in order to maximize innovation and learning in organizations.

REFERENCES

1   Peters, T. (1992), *Liberation Management*, New York: Alfred A. Knopf.
2   Pearn, M.A., Roderick, C. and Mulrooney, C. (1995), *Learning Organisations in Practice*, Maidenhead: McGraw-Hill.
3   Ball, C. (1991), *Learning Pays*, London: Royal Society of Arts.
4   Ball, C. (1992), *Profitable Learning*, London: Royal Society of Arts.
5   Argyris, C. (1991), 'Teaching smart people how to learn', *Harvard Business Review*, May–June.
6   Senge, P., Roberts, C., Ross, R., Smith, B. and Kleiner, A. (1994), *The Fifth Discipline Fieldbook*, London: Nicholas Brearley.
7   Beckhard, R. and Pritchard, W. (1992), *Changing the Essence: the art of creating and leading fundamental change in organizations*, San Francisco: Jossey-Bass.
8   de Geus, A.P. (1988), 'Planning as learning', *Harvard Business Review*, March–April.
9   Hartley, R.F. (1994), *Management Mistakes and Successes*, New York: Wiley.
10 Semler, R. (1993), *Maverick: the story behind the world's most unusual workplace*, London: Century.

GEOFF MORROW'S BIGGEST MISTAKE

My biggest mistake was flying home to see my children instead of flying to Memphis to see Elvis.

By 1969 I had teamed up with fellow songwriters Chris Arnold and David Martin and we had been extremely fortunate in having Elvis Presley record a couple of our songs. We also had the pleasure of meeting him in a Nashville recording studio. We all got on very well and he asked us to write something else for him. So we went back home and wrote one called 'Let's Be Friends'. The next time I went to New York, I got a call from our US publisher on the morning I was to leave. He said Elvis loved the song and was going to include it in his next film. Meanwhile, would I like to go to Memphis to hear him record it?

I was terribly excited and phoned home to tell my children that I wouldn't be back for a couple of days. Unfortunately, when I spoke to my son, who was seven, he was so jubilant at the fact that he was expecting me home in time for tea that I didn't have the heart to tell him. And it was to be my daughter's fifth birthday the following day.

By the time I put the phone down I had decided not to go to Memphis after all, and called the publisher to let him know.

He told me to take down a phone number – then said it was the number of his psychiatrist and that I should call and try to get him to see me as soon as possible. I think it was at this point I realized I had blown it. I was trying desperately to feel like a great Daddy, but somehow I couldn't. Meanwhile, when I got home, the kids kind of said hello then went off to play in the garden.

A few weeks later, the publisher rang to say that 'Let's Be Friends' was going to be the title track of the next album. Then he told me that the reason that Elvis had asked to see me was because he wanted us to write the entire film score.

I offered to leave for Memphis immediately, but he told me not to bother. Elvis didn't exactly have to wait around for the next time Geoff Morrow decided to visit the States – and to be honest I don't think he would have had much trouble finding other songwriters.

I have to confess that I regret that bad decision even more today than I did 20 years ago. When I think of the total royalties for the movie rights and the performance rights that we missed out on, I could cry. And it's not just the money; who knows where else it might have led?

To this day, I never actually had the nerve to tell my partners the truth, so they will probably find out for the first time via this column – and I should be getting some phone calls from them very soon.

The main lesson is that, if you are lucky, you may get three big opportunities in a lifetime. Sometimes it is two; sometimes only one. The trick is to recognize that opportunity and take advantage of it.

The second lesson is that there has to be a balance between heart and brain. If you haven't got that balance, you can make big mistakes.

Clearly I should have realized that if I had said to my children, 'Hey kids, I'm not coming back for a couple of days, but boy am I going to buy you a huge present', that would have been just as good as far as they were concerned (and probably better).

7

HOW WE CAN LEARN FROM OUR MISTAKES

eming, the great pioneer of total quality management from whom the Japanese learned so much in the postwar years, commented in his book that all human beings are born with intrinsic motivation, an inner drive to learn, to take pride in their work, to experiment and to improve.[1] This philosophy also lies at the foundation of much of our work as described in *Learning Organisations in Practice*.[2]

For many people the issue is not that they are unable to learn more effectively but that their learning has been blocked by bad experiences in the past, both during formal education and also formal training at work. One effect of such experiences is that they reduce their level of personal confidence and the associated belief that they can learn. These experiences also lead to a lack of opportunity to develop strategies for coping with situations where learning is needed, and opportunities to succeed in a learning environment.

> Anyone can make mistakes, but only fools persist in their error.
>
> Cicero (44–43 BC)

There are practical things we can all do to help overcome these blocks. In this chapter we explore ten ways to help us learn better from experience in general, and from mistakes in particular. They are based on our model of mistake making developed from the research we described in Chapter 3. Figure 7.1 summarizes this model, and the ten ways of improving our ability to learn from mistakes.

These ten ways can help each one of us to make the most of our personal experiences and to grasp every opportunity and avenue of learning. Ultimately they can help us to become lifelong learners.

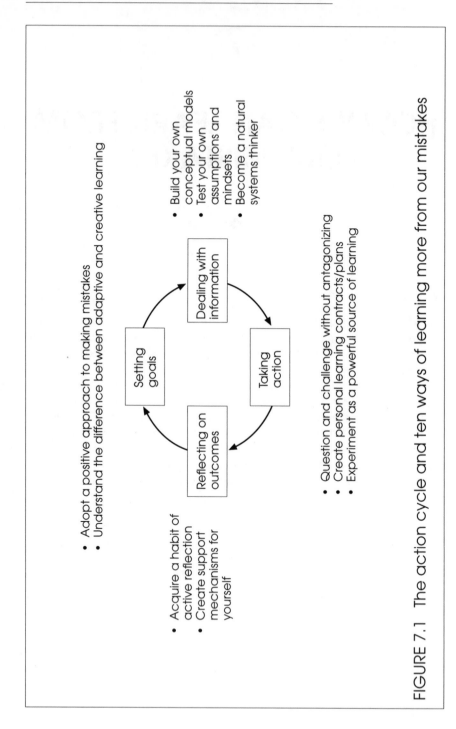

FIGURE 7.1   The action cycle and ten ways of learning more from our mistakes

1 ADOPT A POSITIVE APPROACH TO MAKING MISTAKES

We must understand that mistake making is essential to effective learning. Otherwise we tend to rely on past experience and tried and tested ways of doing things as the sole basis for learning. The adage 'nothing ventured, nothing gained' has considerable merit. Conventional wisdom also tells us that you cannot stumble if you are not moving.

It is important to understand how mistakes can help us to learn. There are two steps you can take:

O   Describe your mistakes as objectively and unemotionally as possible.
O   Understand the way you learn.

Being able to describe the kinds of mistakes to which you are prone helps you to analyse, understand and learn from your mistakes. Having a neutral, non-judgemental way of talking and thinking about mistakes is certainly a help. Without a neutral language we naturally tend to use the language of blame, rather than gain. When we think in terms of blame it is difficult to develop our own awareness. We can more consciously self-manage our own learning by being aware of the mistakes we tend to make.

This can be supported further by being aware of the way we learn. There are different ways of understanding learning styles – for example, the learning styles questionnaire developed by Peter Honey and Alan Mumford, or the adaptation–innovation inventory developed by Michael Kirton. Both these instruments are tools to help people better understand the way they tend to approach learning situations. Tools like these give insights to the learner, which can give him or her more conscious control of learning. They enable us to be more aware of how effectively we are learning and help us keep track of progress.

Remember that if you are not making mistakes then your capacity to learn is not being fully utilized. Do not be afraid not to succeed, but be sure that you can learn from it. If you cannot obtain any kind of feedback or evaluation that will enable you to improve your performance then the experience will merely be depressing and demotivating. Sim Sitkin, an academic from the business school at Texas University, calls the kind of failure from which one can learn 'systemic failure'.[3] Alternative terms are constructive failure or strategic failure.

If you have not already done so, use the practical exercises in Chapters 1–3 (pp.17, 39 and 74) to gain some insights into the context and type of mistakes you make.

2 UNDERSTAND THE DIFFERENCE BETWEEN ADAPTIVE AND CREATIVE LEARNING

The important issue for each of us is how to learn better from experience and how to harness the positive power of mistakes. In order to do that we need to distinguish between two kinds of learning.

> The reasonable man adapts himself to the world: the unreasonable one persists in trying to adapt the world to himself. Therefore, all progress depends on the unreasonable man.
>
> George Bernard Shaw, *Man and Superman* (1903)
> 'Maxims for Revolutionists: Reason'

For us as individual learners, as indeed for organizations, there is an important distinction between adaptive learning and creative learning. Adaptive learning operates within an accepted framework and it tends to be reactive and deductive. Adaptive learning involves the creation of new conclusions within accepted and known frameworks. This kind of learning can be very important and some of the lessons are subtle. Examples of adaptive learning include:

○   the gradual improvement to the internal combustion engine over many decades
○   the evolution of rocket propulsion
○   the progressive gains in power to weight ratios in aircraft engines
○   refinements in ease of use for cameras
○   increasing power of laptop computers
○   incremental gains in capacity to store and retrieve data.

The important words here are gradual, evolution, progressive, refinement, and incremental. By contrast, creative learning actually shifts the established framework and gives us a fresh way of looking at old or established problems. Examples of creative learning include:

○   seeing employees as internal customers for the first time
○   the radical shift from photochemical image making to digitized imaging
○   the rotary engine as an alternative to the internal combustion engine
○   the rejection of long-established passive suspension in favour of 'intelligent' suspension for road vehicles
○   completely redesigning the production of newspapers with the aid of computers
○   replacing hot metal printing
○   interpreting markets as global rather than national

○   innovative new solutions to old problems, e.g. Gortex, Post-its
○   creating complete new markets for products that never previously
       existed, e.g. mobile telecommunications.

The important words here are seeing for the first time, radical shift, alternative, rejection of long-established, innovative. It is creative learning we
often see in the development of completely new products or services. Creative learning invariably involves a shift of mindset, or way of thinking. It
is like Kirton's innovative thinking style, or De Bono's lateral thinking.

Some people find one kind more natural to them than the other. You
can, of course, make mistakes in the adaptive mould, but they are more
likely to be seen as constructive and may be less severely dealt with than
those that challenge conventional thinking on 'the way we do things
around here'. Mistakes which come from creative thinking may be potentially more powerful, but they are also likely to be more threatening for
those that support the status quo. Mavericks and renegades, unless they
are in an environment that encourages such behaviour, may need to learn
social and political skills that enable them to survive in a conservative
environment. Without these skills of influencing, radical thinkers are
unlikely to survive long enough to be able to change things. Too often the
price is that the natural innovator is forced to leave the organization most
in need of new ideas. Mavericks often find a more natural home in new
entrepreneurial (start-up) organizations where there are few rules and
bureaucratic (and stifling) systems have not yet been developed.

Now try Exercise 7.1 (p.166).

3 EXPERIMENT AS A POWERFUL SOURCE OF LEARNING

Much has been written on the subject of learning from experience. It is
widely known that things almost never work as neatly and predictably in
practice as they are described in manuals, training courses and in the
advice of experts. The enduring popularity of books such as Peters and
Waterman's *In Search of Excellence* lies precisely in the attraction and
insights of experience rather than theory and advice from experts. Action
learning is based on this important idea. More can be made from a positive approach to mistakes and to learning from experience with the aid of
mentors,[4] support groups, planned reflection and learning logs.[5,6,7]

> If you want people to learn a new way of thinking, don't bother trying to
> teach them.
>
> Buckminster Fuller (quoted by Senge *et al.*, 1994, p.28)

Here are some thoughts on experimenting as a way of life:

○   If you never try you will never know.

○   Careful and cautious steps in a new direction can lead to major changes of direction.

○   Not experimenting tends to result in playing safe and a reluctance to explore new opportunities.

○   Reckless, unthinking experimentation usually has disastrous results.

○   Experimenting can be done safely through learning laboratories, mental models, scenario planning, and other techniques.

○   Experimenting in ways that do not have dire and critical consequences for the individual or the organization should always be encouraged.

○   Intelligent experimenting should be incorporated into organizational goals, corporate culture and personal development plans.

Experiments are the basis of 'intelligent failure' and they can help us to discover what doesn't work, as well as what does! They can also lead to unexpected results. For example, the discovery of penicillin was an unexpected result of experimentation. It was essentially a mistake – a mistake that has improved the lives of millions of people. We may not have the opportunity to develop a new 'wonderdrug' through our experimentation, but we all have the opportunity to experiment and try out new things in our working and personal lives – and who knows where that could lead? The only thing that is certain about intelligent experimentation is that if you don't try, you will never know.

4 BUILD YOUR OWN CONCEPTUAL MODELS

Human beings tend to make sense of the world by developing general 'theories' of how the world works, and testing and refining these theories through experience. When we learn something new, we integrate new knowledge with what we already know to progressively build up conceptual models of how the world works. The conceptual models – or mental models – exist in our heads and are not always made explicit.

The learning cycle is a model which emphasizes the process we use to make sense of the world, and is very helpful in making that process more explicit. We have developed a practical aid based on the learning cycle, called the learning spiral (see Figure 7.2). The learning spiral provides a way to build meaningful conceptual models, to build on experience, and make this explicit.

There are five main stages in the learning spiral. First, do something. It can be anything – take a decision, some form of action, or something

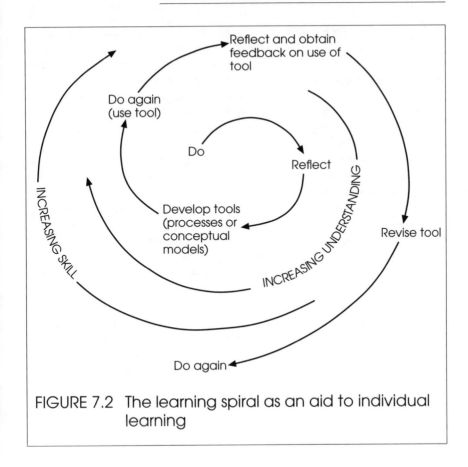

FIGURE 7.2   The learning spiral as an aid to individual learning

familiar but done in a different way. Examples could include trying to persuade through negotiation rather than use authority, or try out real coaching skills. Second, reflect on how it went and, where possible, obtain feedback from people affected or observers (e.g. what your mistakes were, how they occurred). Third, build a simple model for how to do it better next time based on your mistakes and experience. It can be anything you like. Possibilities include checklists, diagrams, flowcharts, mnemonics. The challenge is to try and capture in terms that are appropriate to you, given the situation you find yourself in, exactly what it is you should be doing to get what you are learning right. In effect you are writing advice to yourself about how to do something. The process works best if you avoid (or ignore) theoretical input at the outset.

The fourth stage involves trying out the task again, but this time with the support of your new 'model'. As before, reflect on how well it went, obtain feedback where possible, and revise your model in the light of mistakes and other experience. It may be helpful at this stage, but only at this stage, to seek more 'expert' advice on your model by additional reading, showing it to others, including training and development specialists. Do not, however, include anything that does not make sense to you in the light of experience. After this again try your targeted behaviour or action, but this time guided by the revised model.

The reason the process is a spiral rather than a loop is that you can go on testing and revising as much as you see fit, all the time increasing your skill and understanding.

There are two main strands in the learning spiral. The first increases understanding (by building your own theory or guiding principles) and the second increases your skill in doing or achieving something. Learning begins with developing an understanding of the task in hand, and skill in carrying it out builds on this understanding. Eventually the two overlap and then spiral outwards with one or the other taking prominence as needed.

A feature of the learning spiral by comparison with the learning cycle is that the latter is a closed loop, whereas the learning spiral moves outwards into areas of the unknown. The areas where we do not have full understanding become the springboard for further learning. Some of this further learning may take the form of learning cycles which are attached to the spiral.

Another feature of the learning spiral is its dynamic quality. It is similar in some ways to a tightly coiled spring, which has pressure from within to expand outwards. Like the spring in a clockwork motor (an old-fashioned analogy to be sure) the unwinding must be done in a relatively controlled manner to obtain the desired benefit.

The learning spiral expects that things need not be done or understood perfectly. It expects mistakes to be made. Through reflecting on these mistakes and building them into an 'advisory' model or personal theory which is continually revised in the light of experience, the spiral optimizes learning from mistakes and successes.

The advice you develop for yourself using the learning spiral will be much more powerful than any other model or theory, however sophisticated and elaborate, which has been developed by someone else. This is even the case when compared to the models and theories of experts who make their living from giving advice. Because you have created a model in your own words, based on your own conclusions drawn from your own experience, you are able to achieve what we have called *internalized or deep learning*. This is in contrast to the *surface learning* that is often the result of lectures and more traditional teaching methods typical of so much training. We have also developed a group-based form of the learning spiral which can be a very powerful aid to learning (see Chapter 8).

Here is an example of a personal model (a tool) which I built up progressively in the light of my experience. The tool is designed to improve my public speaking, especially at conferences. I began by listening to tapes of several conference papers I had given. It was a painful experience. I then drew up a list of items that I needed to improve and tried putting them into practice. I reflected on my performance and also on feedback from a public speaking coach. I examined the adequacy of my guidance material and revised it in the light of experience and tried it again at the next public speaking opportunity. Again, I sought feedback on my own performance and also the adequacy of my personal tool to improve my performance. The tool will continue to grow and change as I struggle to improve my performance.

The first part of the tool consists of two diagrams which I created as part of the process of internalizing what for me was most important. I drew on the 'theory' of public speaking but my own experience and mistakes shaped what I needed. Too often, theory and guiding principles (beloved tools of trainers and consultants) are given precedence over personal experience and mistakes, with the result that theory and other people's experience dominates and restricts rather than enhances personal learning. My two guiding principles are shown in Figures 7.3 and 7.4.

My next piece of creative graphics is shown in Figure 7.5. Here I attempt to capture the core process for me personally. The weight at the bottom of the chain threatens to break it. There is a separate list of my weaknesses and vulnerabilities which are not reproduced here. The chain will also break because of the weak links that are personal to me. For each of these I created separate tools. For example, I have created a decision-making and a committing process and a checklist of do's and don'ts when presenting.

This model will continue to grow and evolve. It is based on the learning spiral. It works for me because it:

○ derives from my own experience
○ capitalizes on the mistakes I have made
○ is expressed in my own words
○ uses concepts and graphics created by me
○ avoids jargon
○ meets my personal (rather than general) needs
○ will work because I created it
○ will change as my needs develop.

Above all, it is based largely on my mistakes and my experience and is not shaped first and foremost by the theory and guidance of others.

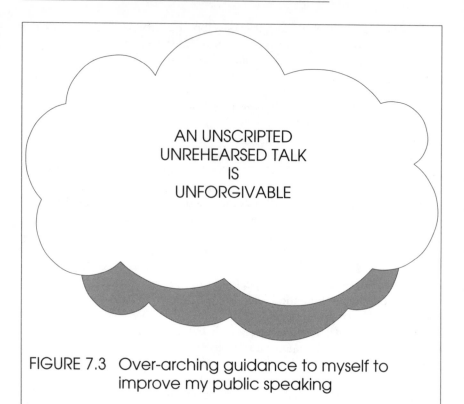

FIGURE 7.3   Over-arching guidance to myself to improve my public speaking

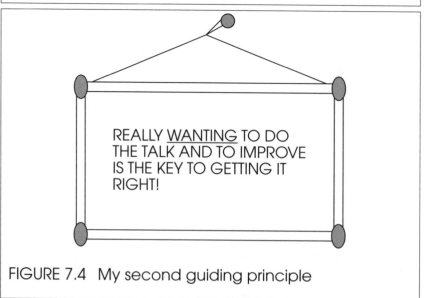

FIGURE 7.4   My second guiding principle

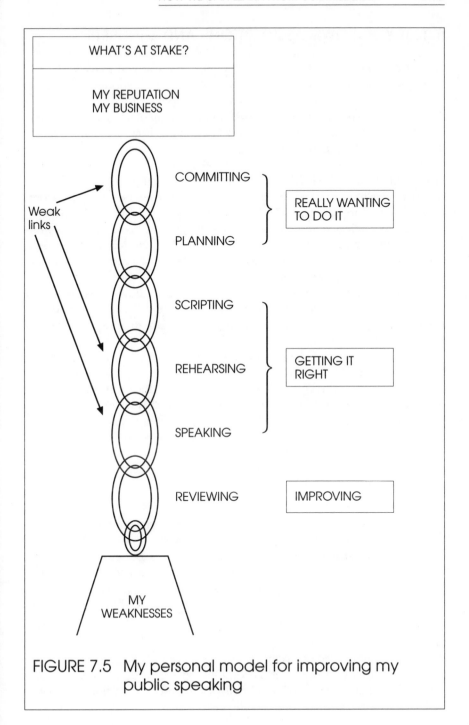

FIGURE 7.5   My personal model for improving my
             public speaking

5 TEST YOUR OWN ASSUMPTIONS AND MINDSETS

One of the most powerful ways of changing the way you think and act is to discover and throw off the restrictions of the mental shortcuts we habitually use, which eventually become mental strait-jackets. These mental shortcuts have been variously called mindsets, mental models or paradigms (see Chapter 2). This section will examine how we can open up these shortcuts for examination.

Mental models are the images, assumptions and stories which we carry in our minds of ourselves, of other people, of institutions and of every aspect of the world. They are usually tacit or unconscious and, therefore, untested and unexamined. They can also be explicit and formalized, although this is less common. One of the biggest problems facing organizations is the lack of opportunity and skill to reflect and learn from experience, which makes it difficult to examine how over-used mental shortcuts may be blinkering or restricting our thinking.

There is a passage in Garcia Marques's famous novel *One Hundred Years of Solitude*, in which peasants who had never seen a steam train come running down the valley shouting: 'Help, help, there is a kitchen on fire, dragging a village behind it.'

A paradigm is an extremely powerful form of mental model. A paradigm has been described as 'a shared set of assumptions, the way we see the world and a set of rules and regulations that establish boundaries and tell us what to do to be successful within those boundaries'.[8] Another example is Harley-Davidson, whose market share for heavy traditional motorcycles in the United States fell from 70 per cent to 5 per cent in just a few years because they just could not believe the new lightweight bikes imported from Japan would ever catch on.[9] (This example is discussed in more detail in Chapter 6.)

Other examples of paradigms or mindsets are:

O   *The earth as the centre of the planetary system*
     So profound was the belief that the sun went round the earth that the original Ptolemaic explanation lasted for nearly 1700 years despite growing evidence (i.e. the discovery of yet more planets!) and ever more elaborate configurations were necessary to maintain the belief. It was even an excommunicatory offence to assert, as did Copernicus, that a simpler explanation would explain the movement of the planets.

O   *Cross-country skis*
     For almost 5,000 years it was believed that longer skis were required in order to go faster. Only in recent decades was it realized that shorter skis would allow a skating, rather than a parallel, movement which was actually faster.

○   *The first office copier*
       Originally rejected by Rank Xerox, the office copier has since become the most profitable invention in the history of business.

○   *The moveable-type printing press*
       The main principles of the printing press, the creation of which was one of the triggers of the Renaissance, remained unchanged for almost 500 years improving only in speed and flexibility. The massive printing industry was radically transformed within a few decades after the invention of the computer.

○   *Captain Cook's invisible boat*
       The South Sea islanders could not see Captain Cook's boat out in the bay because they could not register such an inconceivably large object.

○   *The horseless carriage*
       For a long time after the car was first invented it looked like, and was thought of as, a carriage without a horse.

There are many other examples of blinkered thinking arising from unconscious or unchallenged mindsets:

○   railroad companies not seeing the threat of road haulage
○   heavier than air flight (it cannot happen!)
○   PCs taking over from mainframes (never!)
○   women's right to vote (it'll never catch on!)
○   the sole aim of the enterprise is to maximize profit for shareholders (is it?)
○   the organization as centralized and hierarchical power structure (already changing).

We can see then that we are almost always relying on mindsets, paradigms or mental models to help us deal with the world. It does not matter too much what you call them, but we prefer mindsets.

Mindsets seem to work by filtering incoming experiences so that those which fit with expectations are clearly seen, while others are not seen or are rejected or distorted. Psychologists have long been aware of this phenomenon – they have labelled it selective attention. Mindsets blind us to creative solutions to problems because we find it difficult to think outside our familiar frameworks. These frameworks are so useful to us because they help us make sense of the world quickly and efficiently. However, if we rely only on our familiar frameworks, our mindsets can be very limiting. They can keep us locked into a single vision; they limit our horizons to what we think we can do, how we typically define things, and we see what we are accustomed to seeing and what we know. Years of past success blinkers recognition and acceptance of new ideas which lie out-side the framework that has been the source of success for so long. They can also prevent us from successfully anticipating the future, because we try to discover the future by looking at it through our old paradigms. In short, they lead us to make mistakes, and not necessarily mistakes of the right kind.

Many ideas can have the properties of mindsets. For example, theories, conceptual models, personal beliefs and belief systems, conventional wis-dom, etiquette and social conventions, what is called common sense, habits of thought and action, doctrine, superstitions, stereotypes, preju-dice, orthodoxy and dogma.

Try Exercise 7.2 (p.167) to help you explore the effects of mindsets on your own thinking.

Mindsets are indeed all around us. Sometimes they can be very useful to us in making decisions. The problem with mindsets arises when mental shortcuts are taken unconsciously, or without thought. What we need is a way of bringing our mindsets into the open, so that our thinking can be stretched into new ways of doing things.

Exercise 7.3 (p.168) is a tool for stretching people to think beyond their current mindsets. If you have a situation which requires a new kind of thinking, apply some of these mindset-stretching questions to help you think beyond your current frameworks.

Paradigm testing and stretching should be part of everyone's thinking habits. Often naive and uninformed questioning can throw new light on old problems and should therefore be encouraged rather than frowned upon. For example, 'Why do we do it this way?' or 'Surely there is another way of doing this?' Mindsets are all around us; we do not need to elimi-nate them, but it is essential that we make them explicit, and occasionally challenge them.

6 CREATE SUPPORT MECHANISMS FOR YOURSELF

The main attraction of support groups is that they can provide a safe and supportive environment in which we can talk about and learn from our own mistakes, as well as those of others. In the right group it is possible to be open about mistakes and failures without fear of embarrassment or negative reaction. In this way the mistakes can be analysed and ideas pro-duced for dealing with them. It can be very comforting to hear that other people have had exactly the same experiences as you and that they, like you, do not generally talk about them in public.

The second attraction of support groups or learning sets is that people often prefer to learn with and from others in a collaborative way. This is in sharp contrast to our educational system which places emphasis on individual effort and individual reward, yet few things in life are achieved without cooperation and collaboration. This is being increasingly recognized in the world of work where self-managed teams, project and design teams, and occasionally management teams are rewarded for their joint efforts and not just those who are supposedly in a leadership role. Because of our educational conditioning it is hard to break the mould that learning is a solitary individualistic thing. In some ways, it almost seems like cheating to set out to learn together: Let's remember that it is not!

A good support group comprises 4–6 people, usually from different parts of the organization. It meets on a regular basis (once a month is common). There is usually a structure to the meetings which is mutually agreed by the members. No one is in charge of the group, though members may take it in turn to facilitate the discussions. The characteristics of effective and less effective support groups are shown in Box 1.

BOX 1   THE CHARACTERISTICS OF EFFECTIVE AND LESS EFFECTIVE SUPPORT GROUPS

Effective support groups	*Less effective support groups*
Openness	Game-playing
Honesty	Posturing
Diversity	Defensiveness
Support	Advocacy (imposing views)
Reassurance	Distrust
Feedback	Concealment
Constructive challenge	Aggression
Confidentiality	Destructive feedback
Warmth	Distortion
Rapport	Selective reporting
Mutual respect	Domination
Dialogue	Judgement
Trust	Critical
Acceptance	Stereotyping

Openness and trust need to be consciously built up over the first few meetings. Negotiating and agreeing guiding principles and values is a critical first step. Identifying what the potential benefits for all the members are likely to be, and drawing up a list of quality standards and performance indicators, are also important. Agreeing a mission for the group and a vision of where it wants to be at a specified point in the future also

---

BOX 2   EXAMPLE OF A MISSION AND VALUES CREATED BY A VOLUNTARY SUPPORT GROUP

Our mission

To share knowledge, expertise and experience that will strengthen all our people, and other resources, resulting in a more effective business.

We will do this by:

O   contributing participatively
O   learning together
O   exchanging commercial intelligence.

Our values

O   Supportive to each other
O   Open and truthful
O   Maintain confidentiality
O   Structured meetings with rotating roles
O   Mutually agreed standards and timetables
O   Open and constructive discussion
O   Commitment to our success

---

helps the support group monitor progress. See Box 2 for an example of a mission created by a network of owner-managers of small businesses.

The next step is to agree the structure and process for the meetings and the guiding principles or values to which all members sign up. Agree dates for the first couple of meetings. At the end of each meeting ensure there is time for personal reflection. Periodically, say every three months, carry out a more formal review of how the support group is working.

A variation on support groups is networks. Support groups tend to operate within organizations or within spheres of personal influence and personal contacts. By contrast, networks tend to bring together people from separate organizations, though they can vary greatly in size and in degree of formal structure. We frequently ask groups of people to write down all the networks to which they belong, both formal and informal. A group of ten people can easily identify over 100 networks.

There are many different types of network. Box 3 shows a typical list that is produced by a small group of people when speculating about the power of networks to support learning. One network we facilitated identified four main categories of benefits which they thought were achievable through their network:

BOX 3   CATEGORIES OF INFORMAL AND FORMAL NETWORKS

families	victims
friends	hobbies/interests
sports clubs and activities	alliances
professional associations	partnerships
scientific interest groups	secret societies
researchers	neighbours
universities	e-mail
school (one's children)	community
school (past students)	journeys (regular)
parents	Internet
political groups	forums
campaigning	common-interest groups
support groups	subscriber lists

Sharing

○   resources
○   information (e.g. about customers and markets)
○   different areas of expertise
○   costs.

Combining in order to

○   increase purchasing power
○   gain leverage (e.g. with banks)
○   have lobbying power
○   build new relationships
○   do promotional activity
○   trade together
○   avoid duplication.

Learning together

○   experiences and lessons learned
○   diagnosing needs
○   training together
○   use of consultants
○   reconnaissance (eyes and ears, intelligence gathering).

Mutual support

○   someone to turn to/talk to
○   avoiding isolation.

We asked another network of large companies (interested in business process re-engineering) what they felt was different about learning through networks. They produced the following list:

O   more focus on individual needs
O   voluntary
O   not classroom- or course-based
O   forces you to formulate your own ideas
O   more practical
O   public/social learning
O   self-paced
O   learning through relationships
O   shared values
O   more dialogue
O   you can structure
O   more interactive
O   negotiated agenda.

The members of the network then considered the experience of learning for most people in their own organizations and produced a very different list. They concluded that effective networks have many of the qualities that enhance and stimulate learning. Networks intrinsically possess characteristics that promote and enhance learning. By contrast, when a network fails to work well it takes on many of the features that inhibit and block learning, features which are characteristics of so many organizations which have not created a culture of learning.

The following list captures the reality and daily experience of many people in large bureaucratic organizations which are not learning as well or as fast as they should in an increasingly competitive world.

Rate the extent to which each of the following statements is true of your organization, or your part of it:

Outlives its usefulness	Yes	Partly	No
Selfish reasons predominate	Yes	Partly	No
Stymied by initial success	Yes	Partly	No
Domination by some	Yes	Partly	No
Plagiarism	Yes	Partly	No
Taking more than giving	Yes	Partly	No
Comfort zone/ego trips	Yes	Partly	No
Lack of trust	Yes	Partly	No
Too big, unwieldy	Yes	Partly	No

Social cohesion too strong (no challenge or real debate)	Yes	Partly	No
Barriers to outside world (blinkered thinking)	Yes	Partly	No
Birds of a feather, too like-minded	Yes	Partly	No
Objectives become vague/diffuse	Yes	Partly	No
Cliques and power-bases develop	Yes	Partly	No
Loss of momentum	Yes	Partly	No
Inconsistency	Yes	Partly	No
Talk, don't act	Yes	Partly	No

If many of these statements are true or partly true of your organization, then you are likely to benefit from setting up these kinds of support groups or networks.

7 QUESTION AND CHALLENGE WITHOUT ANTAGONIZING

I keep six honest serving men
(They taught me all I knew):
Their names are What and Why and When
And How and Where and Who.

Rudyard Kipling, 'The Elephant's Child', *The Just-So Stories* (1902)

Some of the most powerful learning comes from asking questions. Questions come to mind when people are not sure of something or there is a gap in their knowledge. Questions also arise where people cannot see the link between things or cannot see why something should be done in the way they are being asked to do it. All too often these important questions are not made public, but stay in people's heads. There are many reasons for this which we cannot attempt to list exhaustively. However, they include: fear of looking stupid; not wanting to slow down the process; reluctance to irritate other people; bad experiences in the past; learned passivity in the presence of superiors or experts; and lack of skill in formulating effective questions or formulating them in time.

There are two main issues here. The first is to learn to have the confidence to ask those kinds of questions which are most conducive to aid learning. The second is to have the skill to do this – the skilled questioner asks different kinds of questions in different contexts and understands the importance of keeping the person being questioned engaged and motivated to respond.

To fail to engage them or keep them engaged can build obstacles to learning that become higher with the passage of time. We have developed a tried and tested process to help people to learn how to use questions to develop their own understanding on a more systematic basis,[10] which we will summarize here. This process provides guidance as to what types of question to ask and how to ask them. At the core of the technique are five broad questions (see Box 4). We call these questions the keys to understanding.

BOX 4   THE KEYS TO UNDERSTANDING: FIVE TYPES OF QUESTION WHICH AID LEARNING

Purpose questions
About the purpose or possible purposes of something

Viewpoint questions
How something might look or be seen from the viewpoint of a specified group

Comparison questions
How something compares and contrasts with something else

Problem questions
What problems might arise or might prevent success

Checking questions
How you can check that you have understood or got something right

---

The purpose questions work by trying to clarify the actual purpose or objective which may not be clear, or has not been clearly articulated. Looking at the issue from the (specified) viewpoints of others, and comparing and contrasting the issue with things with which the individual is already familiar, further expands the range of ideas available to the individual. When the individual begins to think about problems that might occur, he or she begins to focus more on difficulties that might have to be overcome. Finally, the questioner tries to identify the checks that would constitute successful grasp of an issue or a task to be performed. The sequencing of questions is important with a purpose question nearly always coming first, if necessary followed by viewpoint and comparison questions. Figure 7.6 shows how the questions are related.

Although the set of five keys works well and is easy to remember, other categories of questions could be added, for example:

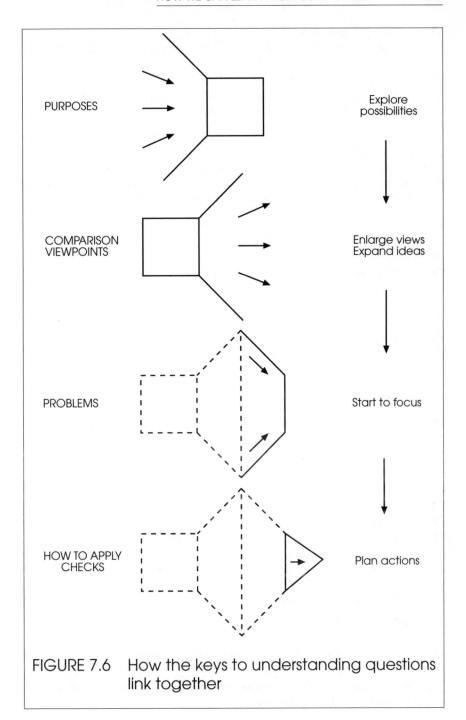

FIGURE 7.6   How the keys to understanding questions
link together

O   *What if? questions*
       For example, what if our competitors doubled capacity and
       halved their prices overnight?
O   *Consequence questions*
       For example, what would be the consequences if we did not
       assure quality in everything we did?

What if? and consequence questions could be seen as special instances of
problem questions.

   The keys are the types of question that are effective in helping people
develop their understanding of an issue. How then should the questions
be put? The key questions are usually expressed as follows.

Purpose questions take the form:

O   What possible reasons . . .?
O   What possible purposes could be served . . .?
O   Why does . . .?

Viewpoint questions take the form:

O   How is A seen by B?
O   How would A be viewed by B?
O   How does A look to B?

Comparison questions take the form:

O   In what ways is A similar to and different from B?
O   How does A contrast with B?
O   What are the differences between A and B? What are the similar-
       ities?

Problem questions take the form:

O   What could go wrong?
O   What would happen if we were not successful?
O   What could prevent us being successful?
O   What are the possible consequences of not succeeding?

Checking questions take the form:

O   How could we tell if we were succeeding?
O   How could we tell if we were getting it right?
O   How could we tell if we were making progress?

The keys to understanding questions, when applied to the development of
safety at work, would take the form:

○   What possible purposes could be served by a safety policy?
○   How does safety at work compare with safety in the home? What is similar? What is different?
○   How do safety issues look from the viewpoint of (a) the community, (b) one's family?
○   From a safety point of view, what *can* go wrong?
○   How could we tell if a safety policy was *really* working well?

These questions work very well on the basis of a structured group discussion where the individuals are encouraged and supported to brainstorm freely before using the outputs to help them reach conclusions or plan action. The keys to understanding also function well as an informal model for individuals to guide their questioning. Individuals and groups can easily work out their own keys using the principles of the learning spiral.

CREATING LEARNING CONVERSATIONS

Asking questions is an important part of a learning conversation, where there is open examination of the issues, and there is a natural balance of advocacy and enquiry. These kinds of learning conversations have been described as 'dialogue'.[11] There is a very important distinction to be made between advocacy and dialogue.

Advocacy occurs when we believe we know exactly what the other person is saying, or is intending to say, and we set about the task of persuading that person to our own point of view. Dialogue, on the other hand, occurs when we do not make assumptions about the other person's point of view and set out to try and understand exactly what it is that they are saying or thinking.

For dialogue, or genuine learning conversations, to occur, it is important to balance enquiry and advocacy. We are often well trained and practised in advocacy, but advocacy without enquiry can block a genuine learning conversation. Skilled dialogue can open up our thinking processes to examination.

There are four basic modes of interaction based on combinations of advocacy and enquiry.

○   *Telling* – testing, dictating, asserting, explaining
       (high advocacy, low enquiry)
○   *Generating* – skilful discussion, dialogue, politicking
       (high advocacy, high enquiry)
○   *Asking* – interrogating, clarifying, interviewing
○   (high enquiry, low advocacy)
○   *Observing* – bystanding, sensing, withdrawing
       (low enquiry, low advocacy).

To strengthen advocacy make your thinking processes visible and publicly test your assumptions and conclusions. For improved enquiry individual learners need to ask others to make their thinking processes visible and to compare the assumptions being made.

USING THE LADDER OF INFERENCE

The ladder of inference is based on a research technique used to help identify our unspoken assumptions which influence behaviour and reactions to situations.[12]

You can use the following questions to help you identify how far up the ladder someone has gone in presenting a point of view to you (Senge et al.).

O   What are the observable data behind the statement?
O   Does everyone agree on what the data are?
O   Can you run me through your reasoning?
O   How did you get from those data to these assumptions?
O   When you said '. . .' did you mean '. . .' (i.e. my interpretation of it)?

Using the ladder of inference can help you to become more aware of your own thinking and reasoning. This is, in fact, a key component of reflection (which we examine in section 9 of this chapter). This awareness helps you to make your thinking and reasoning visible to others (part of advocacy), and encourages you to ask effective questions about the reasoning and thinking of others.

8 CREATE PERSONAL LEARNING CONTRACTS/PLANS/LOGS TO MANAGE YOUR OWN SELF-DEVELOPMENT

It is clear from the above that the learning process is greatly facilitated by using an aid such as a learning contract, and the use of learning logs to encourage the learner on a regular basis to reflect, record and review learning and to monitor progress. The learning album is an attractive alternative; many logs look and can be deadly dull affairs which seriously increase the chances that they will be abandoned. The learning album is essentially a photo album, preferably looseleaf, which takes plastic pockets for 6" × 4" cards. Brief notes can be written on the cards which are inserted in the pockets. From time to time they can be reviewed and rearranged. The card format encourages creativity. Sometimes the learning point can best be captured in the form of a drawing or picture. You can use colour, or take Polaroid photos and insert them into the pockets. The process is essentially the same as with conventional learning logs but learning albums are more fun.

One advantage of the learning album is that the individual is learning to do something that evolves over a series of stages. Instead of trying to describe them, the individual learner can take his or her own photos and attach appropriate notes. Alternatively the learner can photograph critical errors that they are prone to make. The process is limited only by the learner's imagination.

Self-development means that learners are taking the freedom and responsibility for choosing what, how, and when to develop. One very well-known book in this area provides ten examples of practical ways of supporting self-development.[13] The examples divide into two broad approaches: the first focuses on the personal development of the individual, the second on ensuring a tight fit between the development of the individual and the development of the organization.

Self-managed learning has been characterized as strategic learning in contrast to bureaucratic training.[14] It is put forward as a strategic approach which captures the essence of good learning. The self-managing learner adopts an active role; uses formal learning situations for maximum benefit; translates learning across contexts; takes responsibility for his/her own actions; prepares for the future through learning; and maintains a strategic view, linking detail with the bigger picture.

9 ACQUIRE A HABIT OF ACTIVE REFLECTION

Personal reflection slows down and structures our thinking so that we become more aware of our underlying thoughts and assumptions. It also helps us to capture and articulate our thoughts in a way that has meaning for us personally. By contrast, group reflection involves holding conversations where we openly share views and develop knowledge about each other's assumptions and thoughts.

The learning cycle places great emphasis on reflecting, thinking and feeling as being critical to learning. The individual learning cycle is illustrated in Figure 7.7 and the team version in Figure 7.8.

In general one can reflect backwards on what has been experienced, forwards on what might or could be, and finally on the present to obtain a better understanding of what is actually happening. We will examine each of these three different ways of actively reflecting.

A great deal has been written on the subject of reflecting backwards. There is no doubt that putting time aside for reflection on a regular basis is the only way to obtain maximum benefit from learning from past

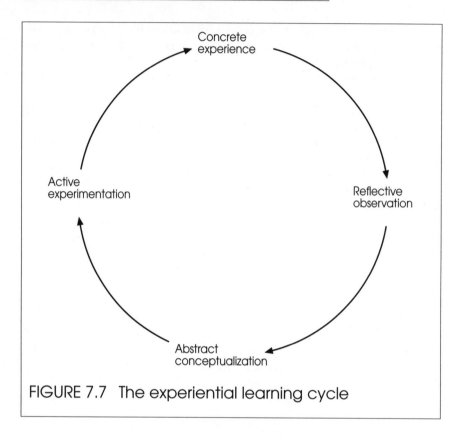

FIGURE 7.7 The experiential learning cycle

experience, including the review of mistakes or errors. Writing down your reflections on a daily basis can become burdensome. In practice, we have found that once or twice a week can easily be sufficient. The questions in Box 5 can be useful ways of focusing your reflection.

BOX 5   ACTIVE REFLECTION: WHAT HAVE I LEARNED?

○   What did I do well today?
○   What did I not do well today?
○   What can I do about it straight away?
○   What can I do about it that will need to take a bit longer?

Two particularly useful questions are:

○   What did I learn today/this week/over the last month?
○   How can I make use of what I have learned?

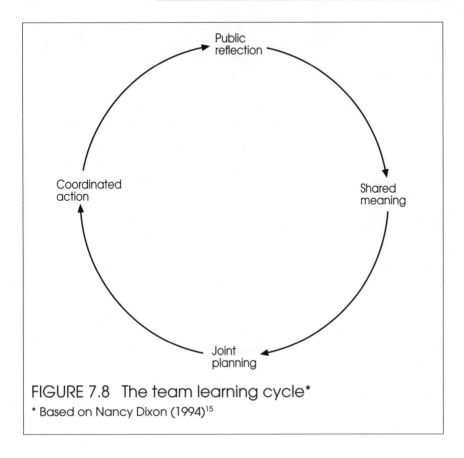

FIGURE 7.8   The team learning cycle*
* Based on Nancy Dixon (1994)[15]

As we have pointed out already, it is much easier to focus on successes than on mistakes. It can be particularly useful to reflect specifically on mistakes that have been made. The key reflection questions from a mistakes point of view are shown in Box 6. The critical mistakes method (a process described in Chapter 9) takes you through a structured sequence of steps which can help you learn from your mistakes.

BOX 6   REFLECTING ON MISTAKES

○   What mistake did I make today/this week/this past month?
○   What kind of mistake was it?
○   Why was it a mistake?
○   What should I do about it?

An important part of reflecting forwards is the attempt to develop a clear personal sense of purpose for yourself: What are you trying to achieve in a given situation/with your career/your life as a whole? The questions in Box 7 can help you to do this.

BOX 7   FORWARD REFLECTION: WHAT AM I TRYING TO ACHIEVE?

Select the questions which will help you identify what you want to achieve. You may have a specific situation in mind, or you can apply these questions more generally to your career or to your life as a whole.

O   If it were possible, what two questions would you most want to ask an oracle? Then attempt to answer those questions as far as you can.

O   What for you personally would be a good scenario, assuming it all works out well? Then write it down.

O   What is your worst nightmare?

O   If you could go back over ten years what would have been a useful future scenario then?

O   What are the most important decisions you face right now?

O   What do you want to have achieved with your career?

O   What constraints will you face in the future?

O   What do you want on your epitaph?

We now describe two techniques which are designed to help you reflect on the present, i.e. what you or others really think.

The Five Whys is a useful way of exploring a current situation or for hunting backwards for the root cause of a recurring problem. Although primarily an aid to team learning, it works well with individual use. It works simply by asking why? five times in succession. You will recognize the technique as the mainstay of all children trying to get to the bottom of something they don't understand.

O	Do your homework.	Why?
O	Because you need to pass your exams.	Why?
O	Because you want to get a good job and make lots of money.	Why?
O	Then you'll be happy.	Why?
O	Because I am telling you!	Why?

The five successive Whys when applied to the answer of the previous question can provide powerful insights to the real thinking behind things we take for granted. Try it on something you have committed to, e.g. 'I am writing a book.'

Left Hand Column (see Figure 7.9) helps you to understand a problem by identifying what you actually said or did (LH) and what you are thinking (RH). It is a method which reveals tacit assumptions causing blockages to learning by analysing a recalled or recorded exchange of views and was developed in the 1970s. It requires a skilled facilitator when working in groups.

10 BECOME A NATURAL SYSTEMS THINKER

One of the best ways to enhance learning is to become a natural systems thinker, not as a formal problem-solving tool but as a language and as a natural way of thinking.

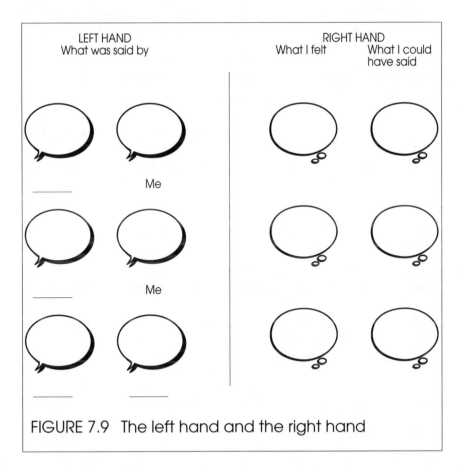

FIGURE 7.9 The left hand and the right hand

> Systems (such as businesses) are bound by invisible fabrics of interrelated actions, which often take years to fully play out their effects on each other . . . systems thinking is a conceptual framework, a body of knowledge that has been developed over the last fifty years to make the full pattern clearer, and to help us to see how to change effectively. (Senge et al.)

Systems thinking is not about solving corporate problems; it is about thinking, and there are specific, simple techniques to use systems thinking in practice.[16] Static mental models are clearly not sufficient to capture the dynamic complexity of contemporary organizations. Systems thinking provides an alternative way of thinking which is analytical, holistic, and pragmatic. It focuses on relationships not parts, patterns not events, and sees causality in terms of circles rather than straight lines.

Systems thinking is designed to reach the non-obvious causes of problems. Systems thinking is about making explicit, and understanding, the interconnectedness of the world around us. In the past, it was a highly specialized skill, used primarily by a few experts. But how can systems thinking help us to learn? Use the questions in Box 8 to help you understand problem situations in systems terms.

But do we need to complicate the situation by thinking about systems? Consider the following seven situations. Do you recognize them?

1   Each employee focuses exclusively on his or her own position in the organization.
2   Whenever things are not going well, it is always someone else's fault.
3   Valued managers are the ones who take aggressive action against the competition.
4   Incidents such as redundancies or poor sales figures are explained by a single cause, like 'the recession'.
5   The business environment is primarily monitored for dramatic or potentially dramatic changes.

BOX 8   PRACTICAL QUESTIONS TO HELP US UNDERSTAND SYSTEMS

O   What are the symptoms and how are they interconnected?
O   Who are the players?
O   What is the driving force in this situation?
O   What are the main limiting factors?
O   What else is needed to fully describe what is happening?

Then, and only then . . .

O   What action needs to be taken?

---

6   There is seldom contact between the different functions within the organization.

7   Members of the top management team never disagree with one another.

These seven situations have been called the seven learning disabilities (Senge et al.), and they are symptoms of not thinking in systems terms. If you recognize any of them, you can benefit from becoming a natural systems thinker.

THE SKILLS OF THE SYSTEMS THINKER

FOCUS ON INTERRELATIONSHIPS, NOT DISCRETE ENTITIES

The systems thinker must break away from simple linear explanations of systemic phenomena, to go beyond straightforward, one-cause, one-effect explanations. Rather, he or she must understand the relationships between the different components of the system, even though these components may be physically separated from one another.

FOCUS ON PROCESSES, NOT STATIC SNAPSHOTS

In addition to looking for interrelationships which may be physically distant, the systems thinker must also learn to be aware of interrelationships between actions or events that are separated by time.

MOVING BEYOND BLAME

If events are explained in simple linear terms, then it becomes very tempting to blame problems on other people or circumstances. A central message of systems thinking is that structure influences behaviour. The 'blame' for a problem often lies within poorly designed systems, rather than with a particular group or individual.

DISTINGUISH DETAIL COMPLEXITY FROM DYNAMIC COMPLEXITY

Dynamic complexity must be distinguished from detail complexity. Detail complexity describes situations where there are a large number of discrete variables to consider in arriving at a decision. Dynamic complexity on the other hand is where the links between cause and effect are subtle and may be separated over time. Dynamic complexity is often likely to be more strategically important than detail complexity.

FOCUS ON AREAS OF HIGH LEVERAGE

Systems thinking demonstrates that the most obvious solutions to a problem do not work and may, in the longer term, add to the problem. The other side of this is that systems thinking can be used to locate 'high leverage' points within a system. Small, appropriately targeted actions can have big effects on a system, and systems thinking is a tool that can help people to identify such actions.

AVOID SYMPTOMATIC SOLUTIONS

Symptomatic solutions address the 'low leverage' points in the system. Such solutions may be tempting because of the promise of a 'quick fix', but in the longer term may only serve to make the problem worse. Symptomatic solutions fail because they do not impact on the cause of a problem, but on the surface effects.

In this chapter we recognized that many people have had their learning blocked by bad experiences in the past. This can have a damaging effect, reducing the level of personal confidence and the opportunities to practise the skills needed to cope with learning situations.

We have explored ten practical ways to help us learn better from experience in general, and from mistakes in particular. These ideas are based on our model of mistake making developed from the research we described in Chapter 3. We have striven to provide you with practical tools for learning more from mistakes. We hope anyone reading this chapter can find something to help them make the most of our personal experiences and to grasp every opportunity and avenue of learning. They are tools for the lifelong learner and they can help us, individually, and the organizations of all kinds to which we are connected.

REFERENCES

1   Deming, W.E. (1986), *Out of the Crisis*, Cambridge: Cambridge University Press.
2   Pearn, M.A., Roderick, C. and Mulrooney, C. (1995), *Learning Organisations in Practice*, Maidenhead: McGraw-Hill.
3   Sitkin, S.B. (1992), 'Learning through failure: the strategy of small losses', *Research in Organisational Behaviour*, 14, pp.231–266.
4   Megginson, D. and Clutterbuck, D. (1995), *Mentoring in Action: a practical guide for managers*, London: Kogan Page.
5   Honey, P. and Mumford, A. (1990), *The Manual of Learning Opportu-*

nities: a learner's guide to using learning opportunities, Maidenhead: Peter Honey.

6 Crofts, A. (1991), 'What did you learn today?', *Transition*, April.

7 Else, J. (1992), 'Learning logs and reflection skills', *Training and Development*, March.

8 Barker, J.A. (1994), *The Business of Paradigms*, London: Harper Business Books.

9 Hartley, R.F. (1994), *Management Mistakes and Successes*, New York: Wiley.

10 Pearn, M.A. and Mulrooney, C. (1995), *Tools for a Learning Organisation*, London: Institute for Personnel and Development.

11 Senge, P., Roberts, C., Ross, R., Smith, B. and Kleiner, A. (1994), *The Fifth Discipline Fieldbook*, London: Nicholas Brearley.

12 Argyris, C. (1990), *Overcoming Organisational Defences*, New York: Allyn and Bacon.

13 Pedler, M., Burgoyne, J., Boydell, T. and Welshman, G. (1990), *Self-development in Organisations*, Maidenhead: McGraw-Hill.

14 Cunningham, I. (1994), *The Wisdom of Strategic Learning: the self-managed learning solution*, Maidenhead: McGraw-Hill.

15 Dixon, N. (1994), *The Organisational Learning Cycle: how we can learn collectively*, Maidenhead: McGraw-Hill.

16 Balle, M. (1994), *Managing with Systems Thinking: making dynamics work for you in business decision-making*, Maidenhead: McGraw-Hill.

EXERCISE 7.1   ADAPTIVE AND CREATIVE THINKING

Place a tick for each item that you think is characteristic of the way you think.

ADAPTIVE THINKING MISTAKES

- ☐ Persisting
- ☐ Perfecting
- ☐ Improving efficiency
- ☐ Refining
- ☐ Consolidating
- ☐ Conserving
- ☐ Depending
- ☐ Cautiousness
- ☐ Confidence

CREATIVE THINKING MISTAKES

- ☐ Experiments
- ☐ Challenging the established order
- ☐ Questioning the unquestionable
- ☐ Restless exploration
- ☐ Constant enquiry
- ☐ Investigating new possibilities
- ☐ Inventing
- ☐ Pioneering
- ☐ Innovating
- ☐ Attacking
- ☐ Seeks breakthroughs

On balance, which column has more ticks? Do the same exercise, this time for the organization you work for. What are the differences? What are the implications?

EXERCISE 7.2   EXAMINING MY MINDSETS

Think of specific examples from your own experience where:

O   the solution to a problem was the opposite to expectation

O   specialized knowledge or training prevented the examination of feasible alternatives

O   the reflex or instinctive reaction produced the wrong result

O   the habitual way of doing something actually prevented a better method being spotted

O   untested assumptions were taken for granted when in fact they were not correct

O   the way things were always done blinkered thinking so that no one thought of trying to do it differently.

Write down your answers and then ask someone else to answer the same questions. Compare your answers with theirs.

Try this analysis on the organization you work for.

EXERCISE 7.3   EIGHT QUESTIONS TO STRETCH YOUR MINDSETS

1   What is impossible now but, if it could be done, would fundamentally change our business? Speculate freely.

2   If the opposite of something we take for granted were true, what would we do? Think of several examples.

3   What shifts in technology are already occurring, but have not yet really changed the way we do things?

4   What is rare today that could become the norm tomorrow?

5   What is exceptional (or difficult) for us, but probably routine for others?

6   What things have we taken for granted in the past, but which have now changed? What things might we now be taking for granted?

7   What do you think ------ (specify a group or function) typically take for granted about you or your function?

8   How would we have to cope if ------ (something that is essential to the organization) did not exist or was not possible?

GERRY COTTLE'S BIGGEST MISTAKE

Gerry Cottle is chairman of Gerry Cottle's Circus, which he started in 1970 with two Shetland ponies, a tent and a lorry. With a partner he toured the villages of Devon and Cornwall, horse-riding, juggling and stilt-walking. By 1974 he had two circuses and a staff of 60 touring Britain; by 1976 they were performing overseas. Despite financial disaster in 1980 when the company went into liquidation, he soon bounced back and today is more successful than ever.

My biggest mistake was taking my circus to Iran in 1978. It was a complete disaster.

It wasn't our first taste of the Middle East. Two years earlier we had been invited to perform for the Sultan of Oman's birthday celebrations and also in Bahrain, and these occasions had been very successful.

Then in 1978 we were invited to Sharjah for four weeks. Our two circuses in England were permanently booked, so we had to set up a third unit, which really overstretched the management.

It meant taking on another 50 people, including ringmasters, artists, musicians, electricians and so on, and cost around £100,000, which was a lot of money in those days.

At the time we thought it was worth it because we had also been invited to perform for the Shah of Iran. We were to open in Tehran, then tour for six months, and they were going to pay us £10,000 a week.

We booked world-class acts at world-class prices. It took three months to set everything up, but this was the job we had been waiting for. The opening site was the Olympic sports stadium in Tehran and they had offered us accommodation in new blocks of apartments. Everything went well in Sharjah, but the apartments in Iran had holes in the ground for lavatories, and the food was served by people wearing filthy rubber gloves. I went to Tehran to troubleshoot, and found our chimpanzees had been kept in their travelling-boxes at the airport for two weeks. I had to give a backhander to the right people to get them out. We were moved to hotels, which they said they would pay for, but somehow the money never appeared. Meanwhile, the lions still had to be fed, the staff had to be paid, and we kept needing spares sent over from the UK because the new stadium was so badly equipped.

We were dealing with a man who was never available. Every time we went to see him we were given a different excuse and told to try again later. On top of it all, the circus had only been running for a couple of weeks when riots broke out. A curfew was imposed from 6pm, and our show didn't start until 8pm, so our audience consisted of government offi-cials and their families, while the general public couldn't get in. We were begging for money, and constantly setting up meetings with people who didn't turn up. For some reason whenever we mentioned money most of them lost their ability to speak English. The rest kept telling us not to panic, the money was on its way, 'God willing'.

He obviously wasn't, because the money never did arrive. Finally I told them we would have to return to the UK, and they responded with all sorts of threats. We managed to get out, but the whole fiasco cost us around £250,000.

We kept our word and paid everybody ourselves, but it milked our business in the UK. As a result, we went into voluntary liquidation in Feb-ruary 1979. It was a dark and dismal period and we lost a lot of credibility and confidence. We had to start all over again, renting other people's tents and animals. But then we had some phenomenally successful tours in the Far East which put us back on our feet.

Ever since, whenever we go abroad, we have always insisted on all costs being paid up front, so only profits are at risk. And while we con-tinue to perform in the Middle East, I don't think we'll ever go back to Iran.

8

FREEDOM TO MAKE MISTAKES: SOME EXAMPLES OF BREAKING WITH CONVENTION

Just as the learning spiral, which we described in Chapter 7, can be used by individual learners, it is even more powerful when used as a group process. An example from a merchant bank in the City of London will serve to illustrate the learning spiral working with a group.

The bank had been formed from the merger of two quite dissimilar banks in the United States, each bringing to the merger different strengths, and making the new bank much stronger in the markets in which it did business. Both banks also brought their own weaknesses and organizational failings with them. Much work had been done to streamline processes and controls but there was still a great deal of ill-discipline and a lack of appropriate controls. The bank was used to making big profits and in the past there had not been a great deal of concern about internal costs and inefficiencies in the system.

The bank had set up a major operation in London and had grown very fast to become one of the central players in the London money markets. Part of its current problems had been uncontrolled growth and many of its internal controls and quality checks had not grown at the same pace. A new chief executive saw the dangers, and could see the increasing competitive pressures from the other main players, and also the growing pressure from external regulators. The bank decided to create a project and quality management team. The team would be made up of young and very able people who were new to banking and would be led by a small management team of experienced bankers. It was thought that this would create a good dynamic for change.

The team of eight quality and project management champions was formed and underwent an intensive programme of training over a six-month period. The programme had been worked out for the team by the human resources manager of the bank in consultation with the management team who had little expertise in this area and tended to accept the HR specialist's advice. The training programmes covered technical knowledge of the bank's processes and products, project management, quality management, as well as interpersonal skills and team working.

After the training period, which also included intensive familiarization with different parts of the bank, the new team went to work entering into collaborative projects around the bank. Many of the initial projects had been identified as necessary from an internal audit and formed part of a strategic action programme.

Despite having trained in persuasion skills, negotiating skills, and working with small groups, as well as general consultation skills, the team of quality champions appeared to have little impact and ran into difficulties with their internal clients with whom they could not cope.

Part of the problem was that they had undergone too much training, too intensively, before they had understood what was required of them. Much of the training had not seemed very relevant to the team at the time and had been forgotten. The second problem was that they had been put into the role of passive recipients of someone else's idea of what they needed to learn. It was a classic example of conventional training, well delivered, but failing to meet the true learning needs of the people for whom it was designed. It was not that the training they had received was irrelevant, but that the recipients were not in a position to judge its usefulness at the time of the training. They had no sense of ownership of their own training and development.

A fresh start was needed and it was decided to use the learning spiral as the basis for identifying and meeting the true learning needs of the group over a twelve-month period. The first phase involved agreeing with the team, in the light of experience and the mistakes that they felt they had made, what were the core competencies that they needed to learn. These were identified as:

O   transferring and embedding learning
O   negotiating and persuading
O   proactive networking
O   constructive challenge
O   bringing about change.

The second step was to provide practical insights into these skills in a safe and supportive environment, which was done by means of a three-day development workshop. One of the objectives of the workshop was to provide insight into the principles of self-development and to begin to build self-development plans for each member of the team. Following the practical exercises and questionnaire each member of the team created a personal development plan. Each person also committed themselves to trying out in real circumstances the particular skills they needed to concentrate on. At the end of a month the team met together to identify the precise skills which needed further development. Not everyone had the same level of interest in each of the skills, but following a series of negotiations, and their feedback and commentary on a series of proposed structures for the 'training event', it was eventually agreed not only what they wanted to learn but also the best manner of achieving the learning. This was an example of customer-led training or, rather, learner-led learning.

The learning event was custom-built to the requirements of the team. Each module followed the same sequence. First, the group was set a realistic and often quite demanding task to be completed either as a group, in pairs or as individuals. The members of the group then reflected on how the exercise had gone, offered feedback if they had been in an observer role, and finally received any further feedback from the two facilitators. Having marshalled the feedback the group then brainstormed, in the light of their experience, a wide range of practical hints and tips for doing better next time.

Having completed this task, the group was given a new exercise to carry out which was similar to the first but on a different topic. Their task was to improve their performance on the exercise, but this time influenced by the draft guidance tool that they had just created. Having completed the task the second time, the group brainstormed additions and modifications to the tool in the light of trying to use it. The draft tool was later lightly edited, typed up and returned to each member of the group.

Over three days this cycle was repeated for each of the five areas in which the group had decided it most needed to learn. In this way they not only increased their understanding of a process by making and recognizing their own mistakes, they also increased their practical skills by developing and using their own tools to support them, which they immediately put into practice. At the end of the three days the new tools were assembled into a guidance manual and used for the following three months. They were then reviewed once more and revised again in the light of using them in live situations. The team found the process much more helpful than the intensive training programme that they had received at the beginning, some of them reporting that the process modelled the way they needed to work with their internal customers over whom they had no authority and who for the most part considered them an inconvenience.

The learning spiral worked in this context because:

○   it is learner led
○   it gives opportunity for early practice
○   it capitalizes on mistakes positively
○   it builds up progressively at a pace controlled by the group
○   the outcomes are built around the experiences of the group
○   the tools are created by means of structured brainstorming
○   the tools are needs led and are progressively modified in the light of use
○   the tools are created in the language of the users
○   the outcomes are owned by the group and not by outsiders or other specialists.

HGV DRIVERS CARRY OUT THEIR OWN ATTITUDE SURVEY

A second example of breaking with convention comes from a leading UK oil company. The company had about a quarter of the market for petroleum products and maintained its own directly employed HGV drivers to distribute its products. Five years previously the tanker drivers numbered over 1,100; they were highly militant and were the second highest paid manual workers in the country. Since then the company had de-recognized the union, and the number of drivers had fallen to just over 400. New terms and conditions had been introduced including flexibility agreements and new operating standards.

The drivers were now delivering more products than the 1,100 drivers used to five years previously, but they were unhappy and uncooperative. The company wanted to introduce a new round of negotiations on terms and conditions and was concerned about low morale, an increase in driver accidents and operational mistakes. One view expressed by some of the drivers was that the operating standards were now too tight, though it was widely recognized that they had in the past been negotiated to levels that were far too generous and that they were not sustainable in today's ever more competitive operating environment. Some of the drivers believed that the mistakes and accidents were being caused by the new standards and by low morale. They were very nervous that the company was going to lay them off and use contract drivers in their place, as had been done by several of the UK oil companies. Management saw the drivers as uncooperative and unwilling to understand.

The management team decided to carry out a consultation with the drivers to find out exactly what they thought about such issues as the operating standards, current terms and conditions, communication between themselves and management, and the possibility of expanding the driver's role. The management team felt that they should carry out this exercise for themselves rather than bring outsiders in to do it for them, though they recognized the need for specialist help in the design and conduct of the consultation, and especially in the interpretation and presentation of the findings. The company was committed to finding ways of working in a more open and collaborative way with its employees, and the drivers were seen as a sensitive group, especially in the light of their militant employee relations history and their feeling of vulnerability because most distribution companies were laying off directly employed drivers in favour of contractors. The company had said it was committed to retaining its directly employed drivers, but the drivers felt they had no reason to trust the company.

We were contracted to help the company carry out this sensitive exercise partly because we offered them an intriguing idea. We argued that it would be a mistake to approach this consultation in a manner similar to those that had been done in the past. A number of attitude surveys had been carried out with the HGV drivers in previous years by external agencies, but somehow the findings did not lead to real changes. The drivers were highly cynical about the surveys, which they saw as attempts at manipulation by management. The company was preaching openness, trust and collaboration, but using an approach that was associated with how things had been done in the past.

We suggested that the management team were not the best people to carry out the consultation. Nor should outside experts, who at least would be neutral. We recommended that the drivers should be equipped with the skills and understanding to carry out the task for themselves and to present their conclusions to the management team.

This was seen by the company as a radical break with tradition which, if successful, would send out a powerful and unambiguous message that things were really changing. It was also seen as very risky because the control of the process would not lie with the management team, and then it could get out of hand. The company could end up worse off than when it started. In a workshop to consider their options, the senior management team examined the pros and cons of allowing the drivers to carry out the sensitive consultation on themselves. The benefits were seen as:

○   a clear act of trust
○   the findings could get closer to the truth
○   drivers would be more open with other drivers conducting the survey

○   the findings would have high credibility
○   the recommendations arising from the findings would not be sold
      back to the rest of the drivers
○   it would be a clear and tangible signal to a new way of working
○   it would be no worse than before.

The management team saw the risks as:

○   unrealistic expectations might be raised among the drivers
○   the data might be unreliable
○   the data could be deliberately exploited and distorted
○   it might result in a return to 'the old order'
○   the whole thing could get out of control.

Despite these risks the management team decided the potential benefits outweighed the risks. The prize for getting it right was considerable. The alternative was to repeat an unsuccessful formula.

Although the drivers might be prepared to carry out the consultation on themselves, some managers and supervisors might not be happy to accept and support the proposition. In order for them to reach their own conclusion as a group that this was a good way to proceed, a two-day workshop was run for the management team. As a group they underwent a series of exercises and group discussions designed to let them come to their own conclusions on the main issues. The workshop culminated in an unequivocal decision by middle managers to let the drivers carry out the consultation with a project team comprising six drivers, one supervisor, and a training officer.

One significant output from the workshop was a statement about the intent and the mechanics of the consultation which was expressed in language that was noticeably fresh and direct, and not couched in the management-speak (as the drivers were accustomed to call it) that characterized all previous communications from the management team. This in itself sent out a signal to the 400 drivers of a change of approach.

The next phase was to recruit the project team and take them through the same series of exercises that the management team had been through, so they could draw their own conclusions about the value of doing the consultation in the manner proposed. When they first arrived at the workshop the six drivers were visibly nervous. This was a new experience for them. They were unused in a work context to attending a workshop for three days in a hotel. They did not really know what was expected of them and were fearful of being shown to be ignorant.

At the end of the first day they realized that they were equal members of the project team and were beginning to feel excited about the prospect. They had also overcome their fears that they might not be able to cope.

They realized they had a crucial role to play and that the rest of the work-shop was designed to equip them with the skills and understanding that was needed to carry out the task and that they would receive whatever support was needed.

Evidence of the drivers' commitment and enthusiasm for the project they had undertaken was captured in the words which took up the whole of a sheet of flipchart paper: 'Get this right and we are on our way again!'

A key output from the drivers' workshop was a mission statement (see Box 1) which was sent to the 400 drivers. It was part of a briefing to encourage all of them to cooperate in what the project team saw as a real opportunity to communicate to management what they felt about a num-ber of important issues that affected them and their relations with manage-ment. They felt nervous of their ability to carry out the task in a professional manner but felt that they needed to get it right otherwise the opportunity might not arise again.

BOX 1   THE MISSION STATEMENT FOR PROJECT STEER

1   To honestly encourage people to talk to us in an open and relaxed manner about the everyday problems we face in deliv-ering our products.

2   We want you to talk to us about such issues as:
   - ○   job satisfaction
   - ○   safety
   - ○   customer service

   and any other issues of concern to you.

3   To gather ideas about how the drivers' job can be developed.

Having brainstormed the pros and cons of different ways of collating the information, the team of drivers decided to run 75 focus groups each facilitated by two members of the project team (always with at least one and often two of the driver members of the project acting as facilitators). The structure of the discussions, the wording of the questions, all the sup-port material including hints and tips for running successful focus groups, and the quality checks were created by the project team in the three-day preparation workshop under the guidance of an external facilitator who used the learning spiral to guide the learning design.

By avoiding theoretical inputs and allowing the drivers to jump straight in and try to write questions or run discussions, the drivers worked out for themselves the kind of help and support they needed. They progressively built up a guidance manual of support material, including sophisticated tools and checklists, to ensure that the whole project ran smoothly and generated truthful findings that they could confidently present to management. As the guidance manual evolved and grew in the light of experience (including doing things wrong) so did the confidence of the drivers in the project team.

The questions that the drivers progressively finalized (in the light of trial and error) were very sophisticated (see Box 2). Other features of the guidance manual created by the drivers' project team included checklists on opening and closing the focus group discussions, the procedure for conducting the discussions as well as practical tips (from their own experience), the procedure for checking and sending the information to a central point, quality assurance measures, things to watch out for, hot-line support, contacts, and materials needed.

BOX 2   THE QUESTIONS POSED BY THE DRIVERS' PROJECT TEAM TO ALL OTHER 400 DRIVERS IN 75 FOCUS GROUP DISCUSSIONS

1   As far as things are now, what are your personal concerns about your job as a driver (or about your job in relation to drivers)?
What would you like to see changed or done differently?

2   What are your main concerns for the future?
What ideas do you have for doing things differently? Think about how the role can be developed.

3   What are the main issues with regard to customers?
What would you like to change?

4   What are your main concerns about safety?
What ideas do you have for improving safety?

5   What are your views about management and communications?
What changes would you like to see?

6   Do you have any other concerns or issues?

The focus groups were run intensively over a six-week period. The data were summarized on to standard forms, lightly edited, subjected to the agreed quality checks, and collated into a dossier for each member of the project team. After all the data had been collated the project team then attended another three-day workshop and jointly analysed and interpreted the data they had assembled under the guidance of a group facilitator. The team learned how to collate and summarize information and subject it to the agreed quality checks. At all times it was emphasized that the members of the team were working as equals and that the output would be presented jointly. They had all understood clearly that their role up to that point was essentially neutral; it was to listen to and to record the views of all the drivers.

Their role now was to summarize the main findings and then, and only then, to try and agree a joint view for the recommendations to be made to the management team.

The findings were presented to senior management by the drivers under five headings, each of which was supported by summaries of what the drivers had said in the focus groups, illustrated with quotations. The headings were:

1   Job/salary security
2   Time pressures and delays
3   Trust, honesty and openness
4   Retail markets
5   Safety.

The main conclusions were expressed in a concise and dignified way, quite unlike the embittered, wary, and sometimes hostile language of preceding years. The conclusion on trust and openness was expressed in these words:

> Drivers want to be listened to and told the truth by managers who are skilled at dealing with people and have the time to do so.

On retail markets the overall conclusion was:

> Problems associated with the customer service centre, delivery site performance by retailers and site developments are leading to distribution inefficiencies, safety and legal problems.

The conclusion was supported by a detailed list of problems and some vivid direct quotes.

The management team were very impressed with the quality and reasoned nature of the findings. An immediate positive response was made and over the next 24 months many of the drivers' recommendations were implemented. Some were not, but reasons for this were clearly communicated to the drivers.

The consultation was a breakthrough both for the drivers and for the management team. The consultation which the drivers ran by themselves showed that they could respond with maturity, and with the professionalism in which they took pride, on complex issues in which they had a vested interest. They demonstrated loyalty to the company, creative capacity and ability to grasp complex issues in a way which they had not always been credited for in the past or which had been obscured behind adversarial mindsets, and the tangle of them-and-us thinking and position taking. The vast majority of the drivers had never before seriously been asked their opinions, other than through attitude questionnaires that they felt were being imposed on them, and they never saw the practical consequences.

For the management team it was a breakthrough because it powerfully demonstrated that by working with, rather than against, groups of employees they could achieve much better results than had been possible in the past. It also gave them the confidence and the desire to work in a collaborative manner on other sensitive issues. The company had taken what it saw as a risk and it paid off. Two years later the same team of drivers was given the task of running another survey on the driver population to assess the effects of the changes that had been made and to assess the current level of morale. This time it was done without the aid of an external facilitator and was a real indication of organizational learning.

The learning spiral and the philosophy of learning through controlled opportunity for error that was used to guide the learning design in the preparation and the interpretation workshops and the whole worked in this context for the following reasons:

O   It recognized that the true experts were the HGV drivers themselves, and not professional attitude survey specialists.
O   The drivers grew dramatically in confidence and skill to carry out the exercise by being allowed to participate without theory and inputs, and to learn from their own mistakes and experience.
O   The drivers acquired early ownership of the total process once they realized that they were allowed to decide how to conduct the survey, and design the whole process including the questions to be asked.
O   The tools and checklists created by the drivers themselves had high validity and credibility by comparison with those normally offered by consultants and specialists.
O   The belief, first by the management team, and subsequently by the drivers, that the results needed to have credibility from a reliable (not necessarily perfect) methodology.

The underlying theme in this project, and indeed the learning spiral approach, is:

The freedom to get it wrong in order to get it really right.

Too often experts, consultants, trainers and managers discourage people from doing wrong by telling, showing and demonstrating. Their own anxiety to avoid mistakes and doing it wrong may actually interfere with natural learning processes and may inhibit acquisition of understanding and/or skills and the development of confidence to learn and take on new tasks. An important feature of the learning spiral approach is controlled opportunity to get things wrong where mistakes are positively used to enhance and deepen learning.

HARNESSING THE POSITIVE POWER OF MISTAKES: THREE CHALLENGES FOR ORGANIZATIONAL LEADERS

In the light of our work on managing mistakes positively to enhance learning, organizational leaders face three important challenges:

O   to accept that the workforce (the members of the organization) always have something important to say and should be listened to in a way that really reflects what they think

O   to demonstrate through their own behaviour that they mean what they say (How many times has this been said before?)

O   to find ways to break with convention that will send powerful signals of the reality of change.

The first challenge is to accept that the workforce does not have to be told everything; that, using appropriate procedures (of the kind described by Pearn, Roderick and Mulrooney[1]), it can produce quality ideas of its own that do not need selling back to them. Most of the time they can work it out for themselves and in a way that has greater credibility than top-down management-speak.

The second challenge is to demonstrate through their own behaviour that they mean what they say. Organizational leaders need to show that they too can make mistakes and can learn from them. If they cannot behave in ways consistent with their work, they would be wiser not to preach those things that they cannot, or choose not to, live up to themselves. The price that they pay is to perpetuate, even to increase, organizational cynicism creating unfertile ground on which to cast the seeds of change.

The third challenge for organizational leaders is to seek opportunities for doing things differently that are in line with the espoused values or need for change that emanates from the organizational leaders themselves. The opportunities should have the following characteristics in order to reap the biggest yield in terms of organizational learning:

O   the process or event should be high profile, i.e. have widespread organizational visibility

O   it should have sufficient complexity to allow scope for significant changes

O   it should be selected or, if not, at least designed in a way that is compatible with the new ideas, i.e. collaboratively, consultatively, customer-focused (if these are the espoused values)

O   it should, where possible, address a long-standing issue or problem in a noticeably different way

O   top management are seen to be closely involved and having changed from their customary way of doing things.

The importance of breaking with convention in this way is that it sends out a powerful and concrete signal that things are being done differently. If the result is beneficial there will be customer demand for more. It will help persuade the doubters and the cynics that there is value in supporting the changes, especially if they have a say in contributing to the implementation of them. The ultimate goal of a break with convention of the kind described here is to encourage people to sit up and take note. The objective is to get people to say: 'That's different, maybe they mean what they say.' The second objective is for people to enjoy the break with tradition so that they want more and want to contribute to their success. The HGV drivers' self-managed attitude survey is one clear example of breaking with convention. Here are two more.

BREAKING WITH CONVENTION

Two examples of conspicuously breaking with convention in which we have played a part involved the recasting of an annual conference and the design and delivery of training in a brewery, including a sensitive consultation with an important group of employees.

A NEW STYLE OF CONFERENCE

The annual European HR conference of a large electronics company was completely revamped and restructured in line with the principles of effective learning, enjoyment and relevance to the delegates as customers. This was particularly appropriate as the theme of the conference was learning as competitive advantage. The conference was later voted the best the company had ever had and became a model for future conferences. One significant change was the break with tradition of having to listen to the great and the good both from within the company and also gurus from outside, who typically in the past had given a series of long presentations. At this conference there was more emphasis on learning from within, and on the emotional and symbolic aspects of learning.

The theme of the conference was learning as competitive advantage. Although the company was frequently cited as one of the world's leading learning organizations, the conference concluded that a true learning organization is perpetually positioned at the other end of the spectrum from Hartley's three Cs of vulnerability, complacency, conservatism and conceit.[2]

Features of the new-style conference included:

O   minimal use of formal presentations
O   high level of active participative learning
O   the use of novel (symbolic and graphic) ways to communicate
O   the 'aspiration hexagon' which summarized the formal/informal learning achievements and learning aspirations of everyone at the conference
O   practical exercises geared to elucidate important aspects of individual, team and organizational learning
O   listening exercises with main customers
O   the building of a learning tower by over 80 people (10 feet high with over 500 components)
O   the symbolic dismantling of the tower
O   the use of action learning projects during the conference
O   emphasis on values, emotion, symbols and a whole person approach to learning.

It was quite unlike HR conferences from previous years and became the standard to beat.

SELF-MANAGED LEARNING IN A BREWERY

The second example of breaking with convention comes from a brewery where restructuring and delayering had resulted in a two-thirds reduction in the workforce over a five-year period. The company was keen to develop a learning culture to help make the best possible use of what it believed was the most technically advanced brewery in Europe, at least as far as the hardware was concerned. A total of £200 million had been invested in new manufacturing technology.

The broad changes in culture and working practices that the company was trying to introduce are summarized in Table 8.1.

For some time the company had experienced difficulty in obtaining cooperation from one of the many unions on site, which had been reduced from 18 separate negotiating units down to three. Years of mistrust on both sides, some justified by events in the past, was impeding progress. The company was not succeeding in conveying its message to the craft unions which had, in terms of numbers and differentials, lost more than other groups.

Part of the problem was that the management team had not significantly changed its own behaviour, even though it espoused new words

TABLE 8.1   Changes in the brewery

FROM	TO
skills no longer needed	new and expanded roles
manual work	mental work
physical tools	conceptual tools – mental models – systems thinking – learning tools
narrowly defined jobs	expanding roles
unchanging work practices	constant change
overtime	annualized hours
custom- and practice-driven	business driven-needs

like openness, trust, empowerment, team working and flexibility. The unions could see their lips moving but little else changing apart from reducing numbers, altered working conditions, and new work roles being offered in place of tightly demarcated jobs. They withdrew cooperation on such issues as the new technology as a source of leverage in their continuing negotiations about terms and conditions.

The brewery management began to realize that, seen from their perspective and history, it was not unreasonable for the unions to be so cautious and fearful. What was needed was more tangible evidence in terms of management behaviour that things really were going to improve.

Gradually the management team began to work on the issue to find conscious and deliberate ways of showing that it meant what it said. For some of the team, especially the longer-established middle managers, this was quite a difficult task. Knowing that one's behaviour should change and understanding the reasons for it is one thing. It is quite another to translate that into daily behaviour, especially in the heat of the moment or when under pressures of the kind that they routinely had to face.

One small change that contributed to winning over the union's acceptance that things were really changing, and not always for the worse, was the new approach adopted for the brewhouse operator training. The training was regarded as crucial, as the operators would be working without routine supervision and for the first time there would be no shift manager to refer to. The role had been considerably widened and it was necessary for them to have a fuller understanding of the technical side of brewing both in computer systems and biochemical terms. Normally the training would have been negotiated with the union and then designed and delivered by the training and development department, relying heavily on lectures and demonstrations with a relatively high cost in failures and dropouts. Now a signal that change was occurring for the better was sent out when the brewhouse operators were invited to specify how they would like to learn to operate the new house.

In small groups brewhouse operators were asked the following question: 'Thinking of all the training you have experienced in the past, how would you like the new brewhouse training to be different?' Their answers are shown in Box 3.

The training and development specialists in the brewery responded by saying: 'OK, we can do it that way.' They then entered into a series of discussions about the contents of the training needed, the level of detail, how each aspect was best learned, and the pace at which to go. The operators provided feedback on a weekly basis and discussed and agreed with the tutors how best to proceed the following week. The operators felt very strongly the desire on the part of the company that they should all learn optimally, whereas training in the past had tended to be mechanistic and seen as an intimidating hurdle with a high failure rate. The brewhouse operators had often known what was wrong with the training programmes in the past, but they had felt powerless to do anything about it. They had not felt empowered to be proactive, nor had their managers been equipped to react positively.

In the light of the success and popularity of the new-style brewhouse operator training programme the union withdrew its non-cooperation, being forced to do so in part by pressure from the members. The self-managed approach to learning (rather than training) is being followed in

---

BOX 3   HOW THE BREWHOUSE OPERATORS SPECIFIED THEIR TRAINING

O   feeling free to question, and having time to do so
O   flexible throughout
O   we build our own agenda
O   we recognize the relevance of what we are learning
O   refreshers and reviews built in
O   we always have an overview
O   no jargon
O   we feel fully involved
O   we focus on challenging problems that make us think
O   we work as a team, everyone has an input
O   our individual needs are acknowledged and met.

other parts of the brewery where considerable amounts of new learning had to be achieved. Another important lesson from the break with tradition was that it taught the managers, especially the more traditional ones, that the operators had brains in their heads and that, if approached in the right way, they were not cynical or apathetic. They could address issues with maturity and the wisdom that comes from years of close experience with what they do, and this was an invaluable asset to the brewery and a key component for its continuing success.

In this chapter we have described four examples of our work with organizations where we have used innovative approaches to create the freedom to make mistakes. Our view is that harnessing the positive power of mistakes sets three challenges for organizational leaders: the workforce must be listened to; leaders must show they mean what they say; and leaders must find ways of breaking with convention. Leaders that meet these three challenges are the ones that harness the positive power of mistakes.

REFERENCES

1 Pearn, M.A., Roderick, C. and Mulrooney, C. (1995), *Learning Organisations in Practice*, Maidenhead: McGraw-Hill.
2 Hartley, R.F. (1994), *Management Mistakes and Successes*, New York: Wiley.

MICHAEL DAY'S
BIGGEST MISTAKE

Michael Day is chairman of The Huge Cheese Company and Britain's only Prevot of the Guilde des Fromagers. His career began in a meat paste factory, then after three miserable years in a merchant bank he was persuaded by his father in 1974 to take over the running of Harvey and Brockless, a cheese delivery firm in Sussex. In 1982 the firm was sold and he set up The Huge Cheese Company, which today has a turnover of £2 million and supplies more than 300 top restaurants, hotels and corporate dining rooms including the Ritz, the Savoy and the Inter-Continental Group.

My biggest mistake was about six years ago, when I took a trip to the Netherlands to see if we could sell to the Dutch prime minister, Ruud Lubbers. We were already supplying Margaret Thatcher and President Mitterrand, and I thought it would be fun if we could sell to all the European leaders. My girlfriend, whom I had met on a blind date at a Masters of Cheese dinner in Switzerland, worked in the Dutch parliament and had set up a meeting with the prime minister's secretary. So I boarded a plane with 30lb of Cheddar and 25lb of Stilton and went to The Hague.

I had to wait outside the parliament building for quite a long time and since I was only in the Netherlands for the weekend I was growing a bit impatient. About half an hour went by and still nobody came. The whole trip seemed futile and I was extremely irritated. Eventually somebody came and took us upstairs. He led us into a spectacular octagonal room overlooking a small lake, and we chatted over a cup of coffee.

I was still thinking this was a big waste of a Saturday morning, wondering who this clot in front of me was and why he had made me wait, when after about five minutes, he said 'What is it you actually want?'

Assuming that he was Ruud Lubbers's secretary, I gave him some cheese as a backhander and asked him to see that the prime minister was given the rest. At this point, my girlfriend said 'This is the prime minister.' I carried on explaining that we were supplying Margaret Thatcher and President Mitterrand, when it suddenly sank in.

With a terrible flush of embarrassment, I realized I had made a complete idiot of myself. I leapt to my feet, said 'Sir, how do you do?', and started stuttering. It just seemed so extraordinary that the three of us were sitting around having a cup of coffee on a Saturday morning, when most prime ministers would be busy running the government or meeting important people.

He obviously regarded it as a bit of light relief and just laughed. I think he quite enjoyed not being recognized and then seeing my embarrassment. I realized he was mortal, like the rest of us, and he certainly had a sense of humour. I have been a fan of Lubbers ever since.

After we left I was slightly hysterical. If I was going to try to sell cheese to him, I should have made sure I recognized the man. I should have done more research, been better prepared. But in some ways, being naive and unaware of his status made it easier. I felt less intimidated because he was such a natural, relaxed person. If I had known who I was going to meet, I would have felt much more stressed.

I wasn't in awe of him because I thought he was the secretary, therefore we were able to talk as equals. In fact, because of the positioning of my cheeses throughout Europe, I was probably quite arrogant.

But while it made me feel humble and foolish, and determined not to be quite so disorganized next time, it has not really changed the way I do business. Most important people find spontaneity quite refreshing. You can usually make them laugh by not behaving in a subservient way.

I don't mean to be impertinent, but I think a little bit of enterprise gets you a lot further than just following in line with everybody else.

9

MANAGING THE POSITIVE POWER OF MISTAKES

It is very difficult to make the kinds of mistake that you can learn from if you stick with custom and practice, with convention and with habitual ways of doing things. Mistakes which arise out of ignorance, carelessness and the lack of proper controls or quality assurance are relatively easy to eliminate, though the amount of effort involved can be considerable. But what happens, for example, when competitors increasingly close in to near-perfect standards of quality and production costs are as low as it is physically possible to make them? Where will competitive differentiation come from? It will come from the capacity to continuously improve processes and to identify and market new products and services faster than your competitors. It will also come from the capacity to respond quicker than your competitors in the face of changes in the external market. In other words, competitive differentiation in an increasingly standardized world will come, as Prahalad and Hamel have argued, from the creation of new ideas and turning them into goods and services faster and better than anyone else.[1] An organization can no longer say with complacency, confidence or even conceit (Hartley[2]) that they have got it right or that things will not change, as they assuredly will, often quicker than they expect.

THE IMPORTANCE OF INVOLVEMENT AND TRUST

Many organizations understand the new reality but they make a classic mistake. They try to sell new ideas and convince others (in most cases this is the workforce as they would see it) by using forms of language and means of communication that are associated with past practices where there has not always been trust and openness between management and the 'workers'. Cynicism has often been endemic and, despite all the talk about new concepts of team work, empowerment and involvement, the behaviour and attitude of management 'as the workforce would see it' has not changed. Above all the management message for change is often delivered in a way that assumes the 'workforce' is passive, knows very little, is reluctant to change, and needs to have everything spelled out for it.

In reality, if they were asked 'What is a better way of working?' it would not be difficult for most work groups to come up with solutions superior to, or at least as good as, their own managers' or the advice of consultants. This is, of course, subject to following an appropriate procedure that builds not only confidence but also competence to ensure a successful outcome, as we described in Chapter 8.

Earlier we stressed the importance of creating an environment of genuine collaboration. Marjorie Parker has usefully identified five starting points for building shared vision which can also provide the basis for collaborative working:[3]

1   telling
2   selling
3   testing
4   consulting
5   co-creating.

As you move from one mode to another there is a combined increase in the capacity required for direction setting and learning and the capacity required for genuine leadership (see Box 1).

Parker's advice is to (i) treat everyone as equal; (ii) seek alignment, not consensus; (iii) among teams, encourage interdependence and diversity; (iv) involve everyone in some way; (v) have people speak only for themselves, and (vi) expect and nurture respect for each other. We would heartily agree with this analysis. We would see co-creating used in conjunction with the learning spiral as a central issue to breaking with convention, a positive vehicle for creating significant change in an environment of scepticism, distrust and apathy.

THIRTY THINGS TO KNOW ABOUT MAKING MISTAKES

By way of summary we think there are thirty things that people and organizations need to know about mistakes:

BOX 1   PARKER'S FIVE STARTING POINTS FOR BUILDING A SHARED VISION

1   Telling is characterized by: *We've got to do this, it's our vision, be excited about it.*

2   Selling is characterized by: *We have the best answer, let's see if we get you to buy in.*

3   Testing is characterized by: *What excites you about this vision, what doesn't?*

4   Consulting is characterized by: *What vision do you recommend we adopt?*

5   Co-creating is characterized by: *Let's create the future we individually and collectively want.*

---

1   We all make mistakes and they are almost always associated with negative emotions.

2   We learn to conceal or ignore our mistakes.

3   Most mistakes, when discovered, are punished (often disproportionately).

4   We learn to avoid making mistakes.

5   If we don't learn from our mistakes, there is little point making them.

6   Lessons can be learned from mistakes that are not easily learned any other way.

7   Punishing a mistake does not always mean a lesson has been learned.

8   There are different kinds of mistakes.

9   Process mistakes are often confused with outcome mistakes.

10   Process mistakes are where ignorance, carelessness, or faulty decisions have led to an undesired outcome.

11   Some outcome mistakes are intelligent (the approach or thinking was right, but the outcome was disappointing or unacceptable).

12   Many outcome mistakes are stupid and could have been avoided (the approach or thinking was wrong and so the outcome was unacceptable).

13   The fear of making mistakes can be so great that all mistakes are avoided and/or discouraged.

14   Some mistakes are the unavoidable consequences of thinking in a creative way, or of innovating and experimenting where the cost of failing is not critical.

15   The pressure to avoid mistakes can be so great in some organizations (where blame cultures exist) that challenge, experiment, and innovation are stifled and sometimes actively discouraged.

16   Not making (or facing up to) mistakes could be a sign that an organization is suffering from the 3 Cs of vulnerability: conservatism, complacency and conceit.

17   We can learn to identify the contexts in which we are most prone to making mistakes.

18   We can learn to identify the types of mistakes we are most likely to make.

19   A neutral language for talking about and classifying our mistakes can help to moderate the negative emotions that can threaten our self-esteem.

20   Many mistakes that are blamed on individuals are often the result of weaknesses in systems or processes.

21   As individuals there are things we can learn to do for ourselves that will help us harness the positive, as opposed to the destructive, power of mistakes.

22   Managers need to provide a supportive environment (including the freedom to make mistakes) where people are challenged and motivated, and mistakes are harnessed for their learning potential rather than dealt with destructively.

23   Managers need to learn to overcome their own fears and emotions when facing up to and dealing with mistakes, their own as well as those of others.

24   Managers need to understand the critical role of mistake making in creative learning, innovation and change.

25   Managers need to learn coaching, counselling, feedback and dialogue skills in order to harness the positive power of mistake making in others.

26   Organizational leaders need to show, in their words and behaviour, that making intelligent mistakes is necessary to a healthy thriving organization.

27   Organizational leaders need to transform their organizations from blame cultures to gain cultures.

28   Organizational leaders need to break with convention and provide controlled opportunity to do things wrong as part of a co-creation process.

FINALLY . . .

29   Not making mistakes is bad for you.

AND ABOVE ALL . . .

30   Making mistakes can be good for you!

REFERENCES

1 Prahalad, C.K. and Hamel, G. (1990), 'The core competence of the organisation', *Harvard Business Review*, May–June, pp.79–91.
2 Hartley, R.F. (1994), *Management Mistakes and Successes*, New York: Wiley.
3 Parker, M. (1990), in Senge et al. (1994), *The Fifth Discipline Fieldbook*, p.327, London: Nicholas Brearley.

MANAGING TO LEARN FROM MISTAKES: A WORKSHOP

This workshop is designed to help managers manage mistakes positively, their own and those of others.

Its aims are:

O   to raise awareness of the value of the lessons that can be learned from mistakes

O   to help participants diagnose the kinds of mistakes they tend to make

O   to develop the skills to deal positively with making mistakes.

The workshop works best with groups of 6–8 people and takes about 6 hours to run. Larger groups can be subdivided. There is a limit to how much change can be achieved within individuals if the surrounding environment and culture of the organization does not value and recognize the importance of positive mistake making.

The introduction to the workshop should be kept to a minimum. The first exercise, Worksheet A, usually elicits from the group most of the points the facilitator might wish to make in an introduction and is usually richer and more meaningful than a planned introduction.

The session has four distinct phases:

O   understanding mistakes
O   using the critical mistakes method
O   handling mistakes positively
      – what are the main behaviours
      – using gain behaviours to talk about mistakes
O   review and reflection.

PROCESS

1   Give out Worksheet A and ask the participants, in pairs, to brain-storm answers to question 1. Collect in all responses using the procedure described in Chapter 7, Box 4, for the keys to under-standing. Then ask them to tackle question 2.

2   Using Worksheet B ask participants to think of a recurring mistake to which they are prone, and write it down as example 1.

     Questions on the pro forma:

     O   Where did the mistake occur?
     O   When did it occur?
     O   What did you do? (If possible, try to capture your words and actions at the time.)
     O   How did you feel about what happened at the time?

      ○   Exactly what were the consequences that made you think of it as a mistake?

      ○   What did you learn?

3   Ask participants to think of one of their bigger mistakes from either their working life or their personal life, and write it down under example 2. If they have time, think of another example and describe as example 3.

4   In pairs, they exchange their stories. Then ask the participants to describe their stories to the rest of the workshop participants, with particular emphasis on their feelings at the time and since.

5   The participants, working in pairs, then help each other classify their mistakes. First, they must decide whether their mistakes fall into one or more of the four broad categories:

      ○   goal-oriented
      ○   information-handling
      ○   action-oriented
      ○   monitoring.

6   Looking at the checklist in Handout 1, what kinds of mistake do their examples fall into? Is there a pattern which emerges? Are their mistakes process mistakes or outcome mistakes? Do they make other kinds of mistake?

7   Ask for a show of hands for each type from the participants and discuss.

8   Hand out Worksheet C and explain the task.

9   Draw up a list on the flipchart of all the feelings described by the participants and discuss.

10   Show Handout 2 and discuss.

11   In groups of three, ask the participants to take it in turns to investigate one of the mistakes already described by one of the others in their group. One of the three should be in an observer role to provide feedback on the balance between blame and gain behaviours.

12   Ask for additional examples of gain and blame behaviours to add to Handout 2.

13   Finally, review and reflect on personal learning, using Worksheet D.

WORKSHEET A: UNDERSTANDING OUR MISTAKES

Q1   What are the possible purposes of talking about mistakes?

Q2   How are *mistakes* different from *regrets?*

WORKSHEET B: CRITICAL MISTAKES METHOD

	EXAMPLE 1	EXAMPLE 2	EXAMPLE 3
Where?			
When?			
What did you do?			
How did you feel?			
Consequences that made you see it as a mistake?			
What did you learn?			

Reproduced from *Ending the Blame Culture* by Michael Pearn, Chris Mulrooney and Tim Payne, Gower, Aldershot.

HANDOUT 1: WHAT KINDS OF MISTAKES DO YOU MAKE?

SETTING GOALS

Defining goals and purpose

Working with unclear or competing goals, or not agreeing goals with others.

INFORMATION HANDLING

Entrenchment

Being overwhelmed by amount of information, and as a result unable to act or decide.

Generalization

Plans and works on the basis of assumptions and generalizations that are not tested.

Selectivity

Concentrating on only a narrow or small part of the available or potentially available information; ignoring potentially useful information.

Blinkered thinking

Acting without regard for consequences or side-effects; more concerned with the present.

TAKING ACTION

Pressure to act

Acts quickly in response to internal or external pressures.

Over-rationalizing

Refusing to act on the basis of gut feel/intuition.

MONITORING

Monitoring

Assumes that things are happening, or will happen, without the need to check or ensure that they are happening.

Self-reflecting

Not reflecting on actions taken, or considering underlying causes of failure or success.

Reproduced from *Ending the Blame Culture* by Michael Pearn, Chris Mulrooney and Tim Payne, Gower, Aldershot.

WORKSHEET C: COPING WITH MISTAKES

1   Think of a time from your work or your personal life when some-one came to tell you about a mistake they had made. Describe it briefly in the box below.

2   Reflect on how you handled this situation. Working in pairs, use the worksheet to review how you reacted. Which kind of behaviour did you show more of in this particular situation?

HANDLING THE EMOTION

3   Think of all the emotions you felt at the time and since. Write them down. Compare your list with the person you are working with. What do you have in common and what is different? If appropriate, take it in turns to say to the rest of the group: 'I make mistakes and this is one of them.' Make sure you describe the mistake fully, using the headings on Worksheet B. Include how you felt at the time and since.

4   Working in a small group, take it in turns to describe your mistake to the others. However, you must *only* respond to the questions other group members put to you. The purpose of this is to practise using gain rather than blame behaviours to talk about mistakes.

Reproduced from *Ending the Blame Culture* by Michael Pearn, Chris Mulrooney and Tim Payne, Gower, Aldershot.

HANDOUT 2: PRACTISING GAIN BEHAVIOURS

We react to mistakes in different ways. Here are some fairly typical ways:

BLAME BEHAVIOURS	GAIN BEHAVIOURS

• judging
  'You were wrong'
• showing emotion
  'I'm furious with you'
• reacting to what you think
  happened
  'Surely you should have . . .'
 	
• blaming people for getting it
  wrong
  'You should never have let this
  happen'
 	
• finding fault
  'You only have yourself to blame'
 	
• focusing on effects
  'This is going to cause enormous
  problems for me'
 	
• assuming the person should feel
  guilty/be contrite
  'You really only have yourself to
  blame'
 	
• seeing mistakes as something that
  must be avoided
  'This must never happen again'
	• exploring
	  'What happened?'
	• remaining calm
	  'Try not to worry about it'
	• finding out what actually
	  happened
	  'Let's take this one step at a
	  time . . .'
	• focusing on the processes
	  that allowed
	  the mistake to happen
	  'What could have been
	  done differently?'
	• providing support
	  'This must be difficult for you
	  but, don't forget, this has
	  happened to us all'
	• focusing on causes
	  'What I want to focus on is
	  all the things that enabled
	  this to happen'
	• assuming the person wants
	  to learn
	  'What are the main lessons
	  for us?'
	• seeing mistakes as part of a
	  learning process
	  'We can learn a lot from this'

OTHER BLAME BEHAVIOURS?	OTHER GAIN BEHAVIOURS?

Reproduced from *Ending the Blame Culture* by Michael Pearn, Chris Mulrooney and Tim Payne, Gower, Aldershot.

WORKSHEET D: REVIEW OF PERSONAL LEARNING

For you, personally, what are the chief lessons (learning points) to emerge from the session?

For you, personally, what are the practical implications of these lessons?

NORMAN ADSETTS' BIGGEST MISTAKE

Norman Adsetts OBE is chairman of Sheffield Insulations Group. After national service and reading philosophy, politics and economics at Oxford, he began his career with Pilkington in 1955, working in marketing and product development. In 1966 he joined Sheffield Insulating, which was founded by his father. He became managing director in 1970 and chairman in 1985. It went public in 1989 and today has a £130 million turnover. Mr Adsetts is also deputy chairman of the Sheffield Development Corporation and is soon to be chairman of Hallam University's board of governors.

My biggest mistake was losing an aeroplane. I joined the RAF in 1950 for two years of national service, during which I was commissioned as an equipment officer. It was my responsibility to keep records of everything in stock at a large flying school.

There was a separate system for aeroplanes, which were normally in the charge of squadron commanders. In the event of a crash, however, the damaged plane was transferred back into the charge of the junior equipment officer and the Air Ministry was advised. It was standard procedure – so simple that nothing could go wrong.

One day we were preparing, with great trepidation, for a visit by the Air Ministry auditors. I still remember the moment when they walked into my office and asked: 'Flying Officer Adsetts, what about this aeroplane?' 'What aeroplane?' I responded. So they took me to the single ledger sheet on which damaged or crashed aircraft were recorded, and pointed out that in my charge was a two-seater Gloucester Meteor jet trainer.

Then they asked me a straightforward and fairly obvious question: 'Where is it?' I was dumbfounded. I wasn't just frightened, I was in a panic, mainly because of the aura of menace the auditors cast before them. You knew they were going to come and go through the accounts and you suspected they would tax you with every single error they found.

You trembled at the knees the moment they walked into your office at the best of times. And now I had committed the ultimate crime: I had lost an aeroplane – which you weren't supposed to do at any time, certainly not in the Royal Air Force when there was a war on.

I could see from the record that it had crashed on take-off and had come into my charge. Eventually, I must have sent it off for repairs. But was there any trace of it? There was not.

I knew I couldn't really have lost it, but I didn't know where it was – and that was just as bad. At best it was careless; at worst, grossly incompetent. The resulting inquiries seemed to last a long time, but eventually – to my relief – the aeroplane was found flying quite happily out of an airbase in West Germany. If it hadn't been found, I might still be paying for it. The reason for holding a junior equipment officer personally responsible for a damaged plane was to emphasize that it was something that deserved particular attention.

I was too young to realize that at the time. I had so many other responsibilities and had made the mistake of assuming that this process was running as smoothly as everything else.

The experience left a lasting impression. It taught me a valuable lesson about paying attention to detail, particularly when dealing with something outside your normal routine, because that is when mistakes are most likely. Don't be misled by your appointment as a manager, at whatever level, into thinking that it means you are supposed to sit at some isolated desk having deep thoughts about strategy. You will have the opportunity to think about policy in the future, but only if you are getting it right in the present – and that means taking care of the details.

THE AUTHORS' MISTAKES

You have read a lot about other peoples' mistakes. Well, here are ours.

MICHAEL PEARN

One of my bigger mistakes in career terms was to stay too long in my first two jobs, both of them for about five years. My learning curve in both jobs was very steep in the first two years but in both cases my personal development plateaued. In effect, I achieved four years of development in about ten years. If I had thought ahead a bit more and had had some career goals at the time (which I sadly lacked) I would have changed jobs as soon as I felt I had outgrown them. There were, of course, other things going on in my life besides my job, but I feel I would have benefited greatly by changing my jobs sooner. Whether I would be the better for it today I do not know.

My recurring mistakes are too numerous to list fully, but here are a few:

- I frequently underestimate the time it will take me to do things
- I overcommit myself
- I write endless lists to delude myself that I am making progress
- I often take on extra work out of sheer vanity at being asked
- I leave things to the last minute and rush to get them done
- I speak to my sons in bullet points
- I reduce everything to bullet-point lists.

CHRIS MULROONEY

One of my recurring mistakes relates to taking on tasks when work is being divided up in meetings. I find myself saying 'I can do that', usually because I feel the work is worth doing and is something that I want to contribute towards. The problem comes when I start to plan the time to do the work in my diary; and I find it's already full! Only then do I realize how difficult it is going to be for me to meet the commitments I have made. I compound this recurring problem by underestimating how long things will take me to do. Combine these two recurring mistakes with a tendency to seek perfection and you have a recipe for late nights!

I made one of my bigger mistakes in buying a house. I really liked the first house I went to see, having decided the time was right to move. I felt very positive about the house – I felt it was perfect for me. So less than an hour after being shown round the very first house that I had seen, I found myself on the phone to the estate agent and was told that the vendor had accepted my offer. It was only later, when I realized that I was going to be left without the carpets and the garden shed that I had planned on, that I knew I needed to step back from my initial enthusiasm and view the situation more coldly.

Taking time to reflect on my own mistakes for this book has helped me to see a strong connection between my recurring mistakes, and one of my bigger mistakes. There is clearly a theme which runs through both these examples: I make mistakes to do with blinkered thinking. That is to say, both these examples involve me focusing more on the present than with thinking through the consequences or side-effects. There is, of course, a fine line between blinkered thinking and an enthusiasm for getting things done. Most of the time I would not change my tendency to 'get involved'. The lesson for me is that I need to be aware that there may be times when I must force myself to take off the blinkers and think through the fuller implications and possible side-effects of decisions.

TIM PAYNE

My biggest mistake was a pivotal moment in my career to date. It was costly to me in terms of opportunities, and nearly cost the business a lot of money at a time when we could ill afford it. It also taught me some valuable lessons.

I had been with the firm a little over a year. I had kept in touch with my previous boss and introduced him to one of the partners. My previous boss was (is) a close friend and 'mentor'. During that year he moved to take up a senior position in the City. Shortly afterwards he approached our firm to tender for some exciting work – designing an assessment centre selection procedure for traders and sales staff.

Tom and I went back a few years and had always enjoyed intellectual debate about psychological theory. We were both interested in an area known as attribution theory . . . how people understand the causes of events . . . and indeed discussed this with respect to traders. There were other discussions of course between myself, the partner and Tom. I spent a week visualizing the pitch (there would be three bank reps) and rehearsing my part. Eventually we were ready. At the meeting I was very relaxed . . . I was in familiar company. I went through my part in a laid-back manner and threw in some references to attribution theory as I knew Tom would like that. However, at one point, I said 'as the three of you know . . .', which was a mistake as there were actually four of them! We left relatively happy that we'd done a good job.

Three days later came the bombshell. We had won the work with one proviso . . . I would not be on the project!! The reasons were that I had come over as (i) too laid-back, and (ii) too academic. I had clearly made some mistakes, mostly I would say to do with selectivity and focusing too much on Tom at the expense of the other potential clients. I certainly learned a valuable lesson there.

WHAT HAVE YOU LEARNED FROM THIS BOOK?

PERSONAL REFLECTION AND FEEDBACK FORM

What are the main points you personally have learned from this book about learning and making mistakes?

What do you consider to be your main mistakes?

What are you going to do?

How should we change this book to make it more helpful to you?

This exercise is intended for your benefit, but we would also love to know what you have learned from this book. If you care to, please send us a copy at the publisher's address. If there is a revised edition of the book, we need to learn from the mistakes we made and, hopefully, our successes.

FURTHER READING

❖

Adler, P.S. and Fulmer, R. (1993), 'Designed for learning: a tale of two auto plants', *Sloan Management Review*, Spring.

Argyris, C. (1990), *Overcoming Organisational Defences*, New York: Allyn and Bacon.

Argyris, C. (1991), 'Teaching smart people how to learn', *Harvard Business Review*, May–June.

Argyris, C. (1994), 'Good communication that blocks learning', *Harvard Business Review*, July–August.

Argyris, C. and Schon, E. (1978), *Organisational Learning*, New York: Addison-Wesley.

Ball, C. (1991), *Learning Pays*, London: Royal Society of Arts.

Ball, C. (1992), *Profitable Learning*, London: Royal Society of Arts.

Balle, M. (1994), *Managing with Systems Thinking: making dynamics work for you in business decision-making*, Maidenhead: McGraw-Hill.

Barker, J.A. (1994), *The Business of Paradigms*, London: Harper Business Books.

Beckhard, R. and Pritchard, W. (1992), *Changing the Essence: the art of creating and leading fundamental change in organizations*, San Francisco: Jossey-Bass.

Bobko, P. and Collela, A. (1994), 'Employee reactions to performance standards: a review and research propositions', *Personnel Psychology*, 47, 1.

Campbell, D.T. (1969), 'Reforms as experiments', *American Psychologist*, 24, pp.409–429.

Collins, J.C. and Porras, J.I. (1991), 'Organisational vision and visionary organisations', *California Management Review*, Fall.

Crofts, A. (1991), 'What did you learn today?', *Transition*, April.

Cunningham, I. (1994), *The Wisdom of Strategic Learning: the self-managed learning solution*, Maidenhead: McGraw-Hill.

de Bono, E. (1987), *Six Thinking Hats*, London: Penguin Books.

de Geus, A.P. (1988), 'Planning as learning', *Harvard Business Review*, March–April.

Deming, W.E. (1986), *Out of the Crisis*, Cambridge: Cambridge University Press.

Dixon, N. (1994), *The Organisational Learning Cycle: how we can learn collectively*, Maidenhead: McGraw-Hill.

Dörner, D. and Schaub, H. (1994), 'Errors in planning and decision-making and the nature of human information-processing', *Applied Psychology: An International Review*, 43, 4.

Else, J. (1992), 'Learning logs and reflection skills', *Training and Development*, March.

Garratt, B. (1990), *Creating a Learning Organisation*, London: Institute of Directors.

Garvin, D.A. (1993), 'Building a learning organisation', *Harvard Business Review*, July–August.

Handy, C. (1993), *Managing the Dream: the learning organisation*, London: Gemini Consulting.

Hartley, R.F. (1994), *Management Mistakes and Successes*, New York: Wiley.

Herriot, P. (1996), 'Stakeholders and survival: who are our clients and can we meet their changing needs?', address to the British Psychological Society's annual occupational psychology conference, 3–5 January, Eastbourne.

Hogan, E.A. and Overmyer-Day, L. (1994), 'The psychology of mergers and acquisitions', in C.L. Cooper and I.T. Robertson (eds) *International Review of Industrial and Organizational Psychology*, Chichester: Wiley.

Honey, P. and Mumford, A. (1990), *The Manual of Learning Opportunities: a learner's guide to using learning opportunities*, Maidenhead: Peter Honey.

Huber, G. (1991), 'Organisational learning: the contributing processes and literatures', *Organisation Science*, 2, 1, pp.88–115.

Huff, A.S. and Schwenk, C. (1990), 'Bias and sense-making in good times and bad', in A.S. Huff (ed.) *Mapping Strategic Thought*, New York: Wiley.

Janis, I.L. (1982), *Groupthink*, 2nd edition, Boston: Houghton Mifflin.

Janis, I.L. and Mann, L. (1977), *Decision-making*, New York: Free Press.

Kirton, M.J. (1994), *Kirton Adaptation-Innovation Inventory*, Hatfield: Occupational Research Centre.

Kolb, D. (1984), *Essential Learning*, New York: Prentice Hall.

Kotter, J.P. (1995), 'Leading change: why transformation efforts fail', *Harvard Business Review*, 73, 2, March–April.

Leonard-Barton, D. (1992), 'The factory as learning laboratory', *Sloan Management Review*, Fall.

Longworth, N. and Davies, W.K. (1996), *Lifelong Learning: new vision, new implications, new roles for people, organizations and communities in the 21st century*, London: Kogan Page.

Margerison, C. (1992), 'Individual development plans', *Management Development Review*, 5, 4, pp.25–31.

Marquardt, M. and Reynolds, A. (1994), *The Global Learning Organisation: gaining competitive advantage through continuous learning*, New York: Irwin.

Megginson, D. and Clutterbuck, D. (1995), *Mentoring in Action: a practical guide for managers*, London: Kogan Page.

Mirvis, P.H. and Berg, D.N. (1977), 'Introduction: failures in organisation development and change', in P.H. Mirvis and D.N. Berg (eds) *Failure in Organisation Development and Change*, pp.1–18, New York: Wiley.

Nonaka, I. (1991), 'The knowledge creating company', *Harvard Business Review*, November–December.

Packard, D. (1995), *The HP Way: how Bill Hewlett and I built our company*, New York: Harper Business.

Parker, M. (1990), in Senge et al. (1994), *The Fifth Discipline Fieldbook*, p.327, London: Nicholas Brearley.

Patrick, J. (1992), *Training: research and practice*, London: Academic Press.

Pearn, M.A. and Mulrooney, C. (1995), *Tools for a Learning Organisation*, London: Institute for Personnel and Development.

Pearn, M.A., Roderick, C. and Mulrooney, C. (1995), *Learning Organisations in Practice*, Maidenhead: McGraw-Hill.

Pedler, M., Burgoyne, J. and Boydell, T. (1992), *The Learning Company*, Maidenhead: McGraw-Hill.

Pedler, M., Burgoyne, J., Boydell, T. and Welshman, G. (1990), *Self-development in Organisations*, Maidenhead: McGraw-Hill.

Peters, T. (1992), *Liberation Management*, New York: Alfred A. Knopf.

Peters, T. and Waterman, R.H. (1982), *In Search of Excellence*, New York: Harper & Row.

Petigrew, A.M. (1985), *The Awakening Giant: continuity and change in ICI*, Oxford: Basil Blackwell.

Piaget, J. (1951), *Play, Dreams and Imitation in Childhood*, London: Routledge.

Prahalad, C.K. and Hamel, G. (1990), 'The core competence of the organisation', *Harvard Business Review*, May–June, pp.79–91.

Reason, J.T. (1990), *Human Error*, New York: Cambridge University Press.

Reger, R. (1990), 'Managerial thought structures and competitive positioning', in Anne Sigismund Huff (ed.) *Mapping Strategic Thought*, Chichester: John Wiley & Sons Ltd.

Revans, R. (1982), 'The enterprise as a learning system', in R. Revans (ed.) *The Origins and Growth of Action Learning*, Bromley: Chartwell and Bratt.

Royal Society of Arts (1994), *Tomorrow's Company: the role of business in a changing world*, London: RSA.

Schein, E. (1993), 'How can an organisation learn faster? The challenge of entering the green room', *Sloan Management Review*, Winter.

Sellen, A.J. (1994), 'Detection of everyday errors', *International Review of Applied Psychology*, 43, 4, pp.475–498.

Sellers, P. (1995), *Fortune Magazine*, 6.

Semler, R. (1993), *Maverick: the story behind the world's most unusual workplace*, London: Century.

Senge, P. (1990), *The Fifth Discipline: the art and practice of the learning organisation*, New York: Doubleday.

Senge, P., Roberts, C., Ross, R., Smith, B. and Kleiner, A. (1994), *The Fifth Discipline Fieldbook*, London: Nicholas Brearley.

Shipper, F. and Manz, C. (1992), 'Employee self-management without formally designated teams – an alternative road to empowerment', *Organisational Dynamics*, Winter, 48–61.

Sitkin, S.B. (1992), 'Learning through failure: the strategy of small losses', *Research in Organisational Behaviour*, 14, pp.231–266.

Stahl, T., Nyhan, B. and D'Aloja, P. (1992), *The Learning Organisation: a vision for human resource development*, EUROTECNET Technical Assistance Office.

Stata, R. (1989), 'Organisational learning: the key to management innovation', *Sloan Management Review*, Spring.

Stewart, T.A. (1991), 'GE keeps those ideas coming in', *Fortune*, 12 August.

Thurbin, P.J. (1994), *Implementing the Learning Organisation: the 17-day programme*, London: FT/Pitman.

Waterman, R.H. (1994), *The Frontiers of Excellence: learning from companies that put people first*, London: Brearley.

Wildavsky, A. (1988), *Searching for Safety*, New Brunswick, NJ: Transaction Books.

INDEX